FOOD FOR THE
EMPEROR

*Recipes of Imperial China with
a dictionary of Chinese Cuisine*
by **JOHN D. KEYS**
and an introduction by **Kee Joon**

GRAMERCY PUBLISHING COMPANY
NEW YORK

FOR KAY
*who maintains that the days of Imperial
China are gone forever—Kaput*

WITH LOVE

This edition published by Gramercy Publishing Company,
a division of Crown Publishers, Inc.,
by arrangement with The Ward Ritchie Press
b c d e f g h

Preface

THE CLASSIC CUISINE OF CHINA *is that of the Peking, or Mandarin, school, the cuisine of the Forbidden City of Imperial China. This cuisine is often ranked equal to that of France, and indeed it was the Cathay of long ago which contributed to the culinary art of France and the rest of Europe, via Marco Polo and other travelers to the East who attended the sumptuous banquets given in the Emperor's palace.*

The intricate and delicate preparations of ingredients in French cooking, such as the making of croquettes or dumplings from minced meat, fish, or poultry; the technique of frying foods in batter; the stuffing of foodstuffs such as squash, eggs, and mushrooms (the Pekingese have gone further to the elegance of stuffing such items as melons and coconuts); the method of cooking eggs into an omelette and occasionally rolling them up with a filling—all these are inheritances from the kitchens of the Imperial palace. Even the stylishness of dressing and serving food, so notable in French cooking, was practiced long before on the cherrywood dining tables of the Mandarins.

In translating these recipes from their original language, care has been taken to exclude those common dishes which have been presented before in the basic Chinese cookbooks so numerously available here in previous years. The result is a compilation of exquisite, unique, and extravagant fare, a representation of the true haute cuisine of Imperial China. The appended dictionary of Chinese foodstuffs is the most complete and accurate glossary of its kind heretofore published in English.

I sincerely feel that the printing of these recipes in English will be a most valuable addition to the annals of occidental gastronomy and fine living.

JOHN D. KEYS

San Francisco

Contents

INTRODUCTION

by KEE JOON

The Imperial Palace Restaurant
Chinatown, San Francisco

Imperial China—the words bring to mind Mandarins in turquoise robes, summer palaces, Buddhist temples, and the Forbidden City. The peculiarly fortunate position of Peking, as regards the supernatural terrestrial influences pertaining to it, have inclined succeeding Chinese monarchs to accept it as a seat of their courts. Here the various Sons of Heaven ruled the land, and administered state banquets of unsurpassed grandeur in palaces of magnificent splendor.

The kitchens of the Imperial menage were of enormous proportion, and a countless variety of dishes were served at each meal. The foods and styles of all Cathay were brought to the Forbidden City, where a cuisine of great perfection was achieved. There was one form of banquet which was to become the highest achievement in celestial cuisine, the Man-Han Feast, a synthesis of the best foods of both Cathay and Manchuria. Three days were required to consume the meal. In sheer grandeur, the repasts of the Peking court are unrivaled in all history except perhaps by those of pre-Cortesian Tenochtitlán.

The Peking chefs had at their disposal a vast selection of local food products. Barley, millet, *kaoliang* (a variety of grain sorghum) and wheat are the grains cultivated in the area. Rice is not a common crop, and it comes as a surprise to many to learn that wheat breads and buns are the "staff" of the Peking diet. Soy beans, maize, sweet potatoes, potatoes, peanuts, and sesame enter into the cuisine.

The lakes about Peking supply a kind of perch called Mandarin fish, bream, and various carp. The Yellow River yields a shad named *samli*, which, in May, ascends the river from the sea to spawn. Goldfish were domesticated by the Chinese centuries ago, and the tanks and small ponds of Mandarin families produced goldfish up to a foot in length, and these were much relished. The Gulf of Chihli supplies crab, shrimp, sharks' fins, and a trepang, or sea-slug that is dried and used in gelatinous soups. The roe of the blackfish, a species of dolphin, is obtained from the Yellow Sea, and is considered a delicacy.

Fruits abound in northern China, and the dining tables of the court were graced with pyramids of pears, persimmons, apples, plums, apricots, peaches, and melons.

The five Imperial seasonings were classified as "salty, sweet, sour, peppery, and spicy." Garlic, ginger, and onions are common seasonings, as in most of the regional styles of Chinese cuisine. A spice powder, known in Chinese as "five-fragrance powder," consists of five aromatic spices. Mustard is often employed. Certain dishes are seasoned with rice-wine lees, or dregs, giving the food a slightly sweet, winey flavor. A yellow soya bean condiment; a preserve made from sesame seeds; and a sauce prepared from plums, apricots, vinegar, and sugar are typical seasonings.

The cooking techniques in the Peking style are numerous; those described here are the most usual.

In the style called "Oil Crackle," the food is first simmered in water until about half-cooked, then drained well so that no moisture remains on the surface of the food. Next the food is deep-fried until lightly browned, drained, and placed in a pan with chopped garlic and onion, salt, wine, a small amount of broth, a dash of vinegar, and a little water chestnut flour. The pan is placed over medium heat and the food is braised quickly for several minutes. This method gives meat a tenderness within and a crispness without, and imparts an onion-and-garlic flavor.

"Soybean-Condiment Crackle" consists of dipping the food, usually fowl or pork, in a batter of egg white and water chestnut flour, deep-frying until half cooked, and draining. Then a small amount of pork lard is heated in a pan, and yellow soya bean condiment and a pinch of sugar are added and cooked until smooth. Wine and a few drops of sesame oil are added, then the deep-fried food is put in, and braised quickly. The meat has a golden yellow color, a smooth tenderness, and the sauce is slightly sweet.

"Broth Crackle," a method most commonly employed for tripe, requires the food to be simmered in water until half-cooked, then drained. Next, the food is placed in a soup tureen, and parboiled sliced green pepper and a seasoning of salt and wine are added. Boiling soup stock is poured over all, resulting in a dish with a green-and-white color scheme, with a clear fresh flavor, crisp and slightly peppery.

In "Onion Crackle," the food is first combined with sliced onion, soya sauce and wine, and allowed to season. Next some garlic is fried in a little oil, and the above mixture is added. After a sprinkling of vinegar and sesame oil, the food is braised for several minutes. Used for beef and lamb, this style produces a tender and fragrant dish, with little sauce.

"Pan Shaking" is used for all foods. After marinating the main ingredient with wine, minced onion, ginger, and salt, it is rolled in wheat flour, then in beaten egg. The pieces are then cooked in hot lard, by shaking the pan constantly, so that all surfaces of the food are lightly browned. The heat is lowered, and a sprinkling of clear stock is added. The shaking and cooking is continued until the liquid is evaporated.

"Wine-Lees Smooth" means to coat the food with egg white and water chestnut flour batter, to deep fry (or poach) and drain. It is then placed in a pan together with rice-wine lees, salt, sugar, and stock. After simmering covered for a while, the sauce is bound with water chestnut flour. Fish and bamboo shoots are often cooked by this method.

A well-known Peking dish is "Phoenix-Tail Shrimp," in which shelled shrimp, whose tails have been left on, are first rolled in wheat flour, then in beaten egg white, then in bread crumbs. They are deep-fried, and served with a small dish of salt and pepper mixed, in which the shrimp are lightly dipped before eating.

The recipe for "Eight-Piece Chicken" first appeared in a cookery book of the Sui Dynasty (ca. A.D. 600). A very young chicken is cut into eight parts, dipped in egg and flour batter seasoned with minced onion and ginger and wine, and deep-fried to a golden brown.

"Foo Yung" is the name of a Chinese bird, and is also the name of the hibiscus flower. The feathers of the bird are similar in color to the petals of the flower, that of a pure white jade. Foods cooked into an omelette of egg whites are given this name of "Foo Yung," and minced chicken breast is most often used. Today in the Cantonese style, the whole egg is used in this dish, and bean sprouts are usually added.

Use is made of a *tan*, or empty earthenware wine jug, to prepare a certain pork dish. Sugar is first caramelized with a little lard in the jug, then onions, ginger, garlic, soya, wine, and fennel are added. Cubes of fat pork are mixed in, then the jug is sealed and baked slowly for three hours, until the pork is tender, when it possesses a winey and earthenware flavor.

One might regard a Peking dish of "Shark's Fin Stewed with Chicken,

Duck, and Pork" as a fine delicacy, yet truly the delicacy of all delicacies is bear's paws. The two front paws of the northern China bear are encased in thick clean mud and baked in hot coals. Afterward, the hard clay shell is broken off, taking away the black hair with it. The meat is then sliced thinly and placed in a large bowl with ham, mushrooms, bamboo shoots, and rich stock. The bowl is placed in a steamer for one hour, then the broth is poured off and the slices of bear meat are drained. The meat is then braised slowly with wine, soya, and sugar, and finally served with a sauce of peanut oil, onion, ginger, fennel, and cinnamon.

The Peking dish which has brought world-wide fame, however, is Peking Roast Duck, with its fragrant, shiny golden skin and tender, white meat. The ducks used for the authentic Peking Roast Duck are fattened in what may seem to be a rather cruel system. Food pellets are made from a paste of wheat, millet, and maize flours, and are force-fed to the ducks morning and night. The ducks are kept in cages, so small that they cannot move about and thereby work off any of their gained weight. In about three months the ducks are fat enough for roasting.

Students of cuisine in Peking are required to take a one-year course devoted entirely to the art of preparing Peking Roast Duck. The first three months of the study are concerned only with the fattening, slaughtering, and cleaning of the fowl. The ducks are slaughtered by breaking the neck, by hand, but leaving it intact. The duck is plucked, singed and drawn, then the entire bird is inflated by forcing air into it. This used to be done by the cook himself blowing into a small hole in the neck; the more recent hygienic method employs a mechanical blower.

Next, after the duck is dipped in boiling water, the entire skin surface is brushed with a syrup of malt sugar, and the fowl is hung up by the neck for an hour or more, until the skin is dry and hard. Again, this used to be done by suspending the duck out on a breezy porch, and is accomplished today with an electric fan.

The duck is then roasted, suspended in an open-mouth oven. It is turned often and roasted for about one hour. Regulation of the oven temperature is important, for if the heat is too low, the skin will not be crisp and succulent; and if too high, the skin will shrink and stretch thin.

Indeed, it is the skin which is relished so much, for when served at a formal meal, the skin will be carefully carved from the duck, in about two-inch squares, and served. The skin is either eaten with the "thousand leaf bread" of the Peking bakeries, or placed on a thin wheat "doily" (similar to a wheat tortilla, only thinner), spread with a sweet condiment made from soya beans, red rice, and garlic, then sprinkled with chopped spring onion, rolled up, and eaten. The flesh of the duck is carved and served as a less-appealing side dish, or else saved for left-overs!

The names of Peking dishes, such as one would see on a restaurant menu, are fancy and poetic. "Crab Protecting Pearls" is a sauté of crabmeat and hard-cooked squab eggs, served in the whole crabshell. "Gold and Silver Duck," thin slices of duck and ham, alternated in a stack of twelve slices; it is placed in a bowl with broth and steamed. "Gold Branches and Jade Leaves," soup with strips of ham and mustard greens. "Butterfly with Threads of Gold," sliced fresh-water snails, sautéed with thin omelette strips.

After the eighteenth century, however, the gourmet capital of China shifted to the south, to Kwangtung province. During the Manchu Dynasty, much concern was given to the southern coast of China, for here the adherents of the overthrown Ming Dynasty defended themselves. The Manchu Court consequently appointed many officials to conquer and control that area. These officials were all provided, of course, with their own chefs, and when most of them were transferred back to the North, many of the cooks chose to remain in the area, because of the superfluity and variety of native foodstuffs. This cannot but remind one of the similar movement in America, when the chefs of the gold-rush tycoons travelled west in the mid-nineteenth century to San Francisco, where they chose to remain in the land of plenty.

These chefs that stayed behind in Kwangtung had previously been trained in the Peking style, and had travelled down through the body of China, where they met and recorded the various central cuisines. The culinary techniques that these cooks taught the natives of Kwangtung, then, were a synthesis of nearly all the cuisines of China, using the classic Peking as a basis.

These chefs centered their activities in the walled city of Canton, situated on the Pearl River eighty miles from the South China Sea. Using the products of the productive regions about them, they rapidly established and enlarged their cuisine, which was to become known as the Cantonese style.

Tea was first imported into England about the year 1667, and from this date to 1834 the East India Company held a monopoly of the trade at Canton. During this period the prosperity of the port increased, and much attention was devoted by the merchants of the city to the pleasures of fine living and dining; thus the cuisine was perfected. When, in the nineteenth century, the many Cantonese laborers were shipped to the west coast of America, the foods of one of the oldest empires of the world were transferred to the newest, where they were to be abused for many years before being fully understood and appreciated.

In the Canton area the richness of the soil, the plentiful moisture, and the superabundance of labor combine to make soil culture a highly developed art. The cultivation of rice is the dominant agricultural occupation, as it serves as the basis of the Cantonese diet. Yams and taro are the next most important crops.

Many kinds of vegetables are raised throughout the region and at all seasons. They include such exotic items as a large white vegetable marrow called "winter melon"; the balsam pear or "bitter melon," with a green wrinkled skin and a bitter, cool flavor, due to the presence of quinine; the brinjal marrow, called "hairy melon," green, with fine white fuzz on the skin; loofah gourd or squash, a member of the cucumber family; roots of the lotus lily; and a green bean which attains the length of three feet!

Fruits abound, among them the *litchi*, a white translucent pulp enclosed in a shell-like red skin; the flavor is sweet, delicate, and very refreshing; when dried and exported, they become the "lichee nuts" popular in the United States. The loose-skinned mandarin orange, indigenous to China, was the forerunner of the small tangerine. Pomelos, mangos, persimmons, bananas, jujubes, and pineapples are plentiful. Peanuts, sesame, and coconuts are grown here, while the best ginger in China comes from Kwangtung province.

The coastline of Kwangtung has many promontories and protected bays, yet despite these natural harbors, fishing has not developed extensively, for the temperature of the ocean is warmer and not so favorable to fish as the cooler seas to the North. Nevertheless, the Cantonese are fond of fish dishes, and import sea delicacies from the rest of China. Sharks' fins, sea tortoise, abalone, trepang, and scallops are obtained from the East China Sea and dried. Although not listed under the heading of fish, swallow's nests are closely linked to the sea, for they are constructed from the saliva of a certain bird, after it has digested seaweed. Rich in protein, swallow's nest is relished in Canton.

Cantonese chefs take into consideration six sensations of taste when they are preparing a dish: sour, sweet, bitter, salty, peppery, and natural, the latter being the unadulterated taste of the raw food itself. In general, the same general seasonings are used as in the Peking style. A much-used seasoning is oyster sauce, a rich red-brown sauce made from fresh oysters. Various dried mushrooms are used, as are several types of tree fungi, known as "snow fungus," "tree ears," "silver ears," etc. Tomato sauce is employed in many Cantonese dishes; indeed, its pronunciation in Cantonese is *kair jup*, a cause for momentary reflection. Curry powder has recently become a favorite seasoning, and is imported.

For years no use was made of cow's milk, either in its natural state or in the form of butter or cheese. But the Cantonese chefs, progressive in every way, have recently made use of butter in some dishes, although as a flavoring additive only.

The Cantonese style is noted for its tea-time snacks and pastries, to which many Cantonese cookbooks are entirely devoted. The powers of invention have been carried to the fullest in this category of the cuisine, and in Canton there are tea-houses whose menus are limited to these delicacies, known in the native language as "dot hearts", something to just touch upon one's appetite.

Today, the Cantonese style of Chinese cuisine is the most famous in China, as well as abroad. We Chinese have a saying, "To be born in Soochow, to dine in Kwangchow"; the former city is famed for its beautiful women, and the latter for the excellence of its cuisine.

I believe that here in America, since World War II, we are experiencing what I choose to term a "second revolution" of Chinese food. For the first time, the cuisine of ancient China is being introduced to the Western people, and I myself have earnestly supported this inauguration here at the Imperial Palace Restaurant. "Ancient eggs, shark's fin soup, bitter melon . . . anything but chop suey" is the proposition which appears at the head of the menu, and authentic dishes from every region of China are offered.

In this enticing cookery book, Mr. Keys has maintained this variety of regional Chinese dishes. From all corners of ancient Cathay, here is a compilation of foods gathered and brought back to the Imperial court by the Emperor's gastronomic officials.

Here indeed is *food for the Emperor!*

其臻

KEE JOON

FOOD FOR THE EMPEROR

Dumplings of Ham & Shrimp in Seasoned Broth
CHING-TONG HAR-KOW

1 lb. fresh shrimp
½ cup chopped ham
1 tsp. salt
3 unbeaten egg whites

1 tbsp. cornstarch
1 tsp. sugar
2 tsp. soya sauce
Rich soup stock

Shell, devein, and wash the shrimps. Mince them together with the ham. Add the salt, egg white, cornstarch, sugar, and soya sauce. Mix well until smooth.

Heat about 3 inches of water in a pan. Form the shrimp mixture into small balls and drop them carefully into the boiling water. Cover and cook gently until they float to the surface. Drain them. It may be necessary to cook the dumplings a few at a time.

Bring clear soup stock to boil and season. Place the shrimp dumplings in a large soup tureen and add the broth.

"In making a mixture you must judge to a nicety what is sweet, sour, bitter, sharp, and salt: you must know which has to be added first, later, and how much of each. This distribution is very complicated but it must be controlled in every detail by addition. The changes which take place in the food after it has been prepared in the dish are so delicate and mysterious that it is impossible to describe them in words."

I YIN, 2000 B.C.

Fillet of Chicken in Whole Coconuts with Button Mushrooms

YE-JEE GAI-YUK

4 small coconuts	½ lb. fresh white button
3 cups sliced chicken meat, uncooked	mushrooms
1½ cup chicken broth	1½ cup rich milk

Carefully saw open the top of each coconut, about ⅓ of the coconut, and save the tops as lids. Discard the coconut milk.

Combine the chicken meat with the whole button mushrooms, and season with salt. Divide the mixture into the four coconuts.

Combine the chicken stock and milk and pour ¾ cup of the mixture into each coconut, or until the coconuts are filled. Replace the lids on the coconuts and bind them with twine, so that the lids are tightly closed.

Support the coconuts upright on a rack in a roasting pan containing 3 inches boiling water. Cover the pan and place over two burners on the top of the stove. Steam the coconuts for 4 to 5 hours, until the chicken is tender. Replenish the water in the pan when necessary.

Remove the twine and support the coconuts in small bowls, serving one to a person.

4

Medallions of Pork with Crabmeat Filling

GUM-CHIN HI-HOP

Pork loin roast, cooked	½ tsp. seasoning powder
Cornstarch	2 tsp. soya sauce
½ cup canned crabmeat	3 egg whites, beaten until frothy
¼ cup chopped fresh mushrooms	Chopped parsley
¼ cup chopped bamboo shoots	

With a sharp knife, cut the cold roast into slices ¼ inch thick. Then cut the slices into 1-inch squares. Cut enough to yield 24 squares. Dust the pork wafers with cornstarch.

Combine the crabmeat, mushrooms, and bamboo shoots. Chop very fine. Add the seasoning powder, 1 teaspoon sifted cornstarch, and the soya sauce. Season with salt.

Spread 12 of the pork squares with the crabmeat mixture. Top them with the remaining 12 wafers, sandwich style. Press gently to make them stick.

Dip each pork medallion in egg white, then fry in deep fat until golden brown. Serve sprinkled with chopped parsley.

"There were forty large crabs, ready dressed with peppers, ginger, garlic, and herbs, and prepared with oil, sauce, and vinegar. They smelled very tasty and promised excellent eating. The two roast ducks were done in the most attractive style. The wine was brought and opened. It was pale green in color and very sweet. Before it was poured into the wine-pot, a jar of cold water was mixed with it to make it milder. It had a very delicate flavor, finer than that of grape wine."

From the novel, *Chin P'ing Mei*
Translated by CLEMENT EGERTON

Duckling Steamed in Fine White Wine

JOW JING CHUEN-AAP

1 tender fat duckling
1 large onion
2 slices fresh ginger root

1 tsp. sugar
1 tbsp. soya sauce
1 cup fine rice wine or sherry

Clean the duckling, but leave it whole. Dry it inside and out with paper towels. Brown it on all sides in heated oil. In cold water rinse the duckling of all oil; drain.

Sprinkle the duckling lightly inside and out with salt. Slice the onion thinly and place inside the duckling together with the ginger. Sew up securely.

Place the duckling in a large bowl. Sprinkle with the sugar and soya sauce, then pour the wine over it.

Place the bowl on a rack in a large pot containing 3 inches boiling water. Cover the pot and steam the duck over low heat for two hours, or until the duckling is tender.

Replenish the water in the pot when necessary.

"Out in the garden in the moonlight, our servant is scraping a golden carp with so much vigor that the scales fly in every direction—perhaps they go as high as heaven. Those beautiful stars up there might be the scales of our fish."

CHANG WOU KIEN, *Before the Repast*

6

Poached Fillet of Fish Stuffed with Pork, Shrimp & Onion

YEW-YUK WUN-TUN

8 small fillets of any white fish
⅓ cup chopped cooked pork
⅓ cup chopped cooked shrimp
⅓ cup minced onion
White wine
Soya sauce

Mix the pork, shrimp, and onion together well, and season with salt. Spread 2 tablespoons of this mixture over each fish fillet. Fold the fillets over once or twice and secure them with toothpicks.

Place the rolled fillets in a shallow pan and add enough water and wine, mixed half-and-half, to barely cover the fish. Add 1 to 2 tablespoons soya sauce. Allow the mixture to stand for 30 minutes.

Place the pan over a gentle fire and heat slowly until the liquid reaches the boiling point, at which time the fish should be cooked. Do not boil.

Remove the fish very carefully from the liquid and arrange on a warm serving dish. Remove the toothpicks.

Pour a small amount of the cooking liquid over the fish, sprinkle with a little salt and pepper, and serve immediately.

"I am sending you some leaves of tea. They come from the tree belonging to the monastery which lies upon the mountain Ou I.

"Take a blue urn of Ni Hung. Fill it with water which has been melted from snow gathered, at sunrise, upon the western slope of the mountain Sou Chan; place this urn over a fire of maple twigs that have been collected from among very old moss, and leave it there just until the water begins to laugh. Then pour it into a cup of Huen Tcha in which you have placed some leaves of this tea, cover the cup with a bit of white silk woven at Houa Chan, and wait until your room is filled with a perfume like that of a garden of Fouen Lo.

"Lift the cup to your lips, then close your eyes. You will be in Paradise."

OUANG TSI (723-737), *to a friend*

Chicken Barbecued with Fragrant Spices

NG-HERNG GAI

1 young chicken of about 3 lb.	1 tsp. fresh ginger root, minced
½ tsp. cinnamon	1 cup chicken broth
½ tsp. cloves powder	Soya sauce
½ tsp. aniseed	Peanut oil
2 tbsp. finely chopped onion	Cornstarch binder

Disjoint the chicken, then chop it with a cleaver into 1-inch pieces, bones included. Mix the chicken in a bowl with ¼ cup soya sauce and allow to marinate for 1 hour, turning occasionally. Drain it well, then brown in hot peanut oil.

Arrange the browned chicken in a shallow baking dish and sprinkle it with the cinnamon, cloves, aniseed, onion, and ginger. Add the chicken broth, cover the dish, and bake it in a moderate oven for about 1 hour, turning several times.

Remove the chicken to a warm serving dish. Add additional chicken broth to the drippings, so that there is 1 cup of liquid. Strain the broth into a saucepan, bring to a boil, and thicken slightly with cornstarch binder. Pour over the chicken.

9

THE FIFTEEN RULES FOR DRINKING

1. Get intoxicated, but don't get helplessly drunk. Drunkenness causes life-long ill-health.
2. Don't lie in a draft when drunk—this brings on fits.
3. Don't lie in the sun when drunk—this way lies madness.
4. Don't lie in the dew when drunk—rheumatism will result.
5. Never force yourself to eat, and never get angry, when you are under the influence of drink, or you will break out in boils. Washing the face in cold water has the same effect.
6. Don't drink on an empty stomach or you will certainly be sick.
7. Never take sweet things with wine.
8. Don't eat pork with wine as this causes convulsions.
9. Don't bathe when you are affected by wine; it is bad for the eyes.
10. Don't ride or jump about, or exert yourself in any way when drunk or you will injure your bones and sinews and undermine your strength.
11. When you recover from a bout of drinking, pause before beginning again; in this way you will avoid adding harm to harm.
12. When drinking don't talk too much. When you know you have done so, it is best to vomit it up at once.
13. When drunk don't get so excited that you scare your soul out of your body for good.
14. If you suffer from bad eyes, avoid drinking or eating to excess.
15. If you see in your wine the reflection of a person not in your range of vision, don't drink it.

From the *Imperial Cookery Book of the Mongol Dynasty*

Beef Stewed in Fruit Sauce

GWOR-JUP NGOW-NAAM

菓
汁
牛
腩

1 large orange	1/3 cup rice wine or sherry
1 tangerine	1 tbsp. A-1 steak sauce
1 large pear	1/4 tsp. cinnamon
2 lb. stewing beef, cut in 1" cubes	1/4 tsp. aniseed
	1/4 tsp. cloves powder
Juice of 1 lemon	1/4 tsp. pepper
4 cloves garlic, minced	1/2 tsp. salt
1 tbsp. sugar	1 tsp. fresh ginger root, minced

Peel the orange and tangerine. Pull the sections of the fruit apart, removing seeds. Skin the pear, seed, and cut into thin slices.

Brown the beef in a Dutch oven together with the garlic. Add the sugar, wine, minced ginger, A-1 sauce, cinnamon, aniseed, cloves powder, pepper, and salt.

Add the orange, tangerine, and pear, then the lemon juice. Stir in 1½ cup boiling water, cover, and simmer gently for 2 to 3 hours, until the beef is extremely tender.

"Some animals are good for food; others are not. But avoid even those which are normally edible if there be anything unnatural in their appearance. Do not eat horse's feet; they have eyes in them at night. A black chicken or sheep with a white head, or a sheep with only a single horn, or a horned horse, should never be used for food. The same rule applies to meat which falls on the ground and does not leave a wet patch, or which is found to be warm after having been left overnight."
From the *Imperial Cookery Book of the Mongol Dynasty*

"Before we sat down to table, one of the guardians of the palace brought us a large copper tub filled with boiling water, into which he plunged some small napkins, and then wringing them out, he presented one to each of us. Linen towels are made use of in this way, hot and smoking, to wipe the hands and face; and the custom of offering them to you after meals and on journeys is universal in China."

M. HUC, *A Journey through the Chinese Empire*, 1854

Stuffed Chinese Black Mushrooms Steamed in Chicken Broth

GUM-CHIN YERNG DOAN-KOO

8 medium Chinese dried
   black mushrooms
¼ cup chopped shrimp
¼ cup chopped onion
½ tsp. minced fresh ginger root
1 tsp. soya sauce

½ tsp. sugar
½ tsp. seasoning powder
Chicken stock
Parsley
White wine

Soak the dried mushrooms in hot water 15 minutes. Drain, wash, and clean, and remove the stems.

Combine the shrimp, onion, and ginger. Mince thoroughly. Add the soya sauce, sugar, and seasoning powder; season with salt. Mix well until smooth.

Place 2 teaspoons of the shrimp mixture on the underside of each mushroom cap; press to stick. Pour ½ inch chicken stock in a large shallow pan; season with white wine. Place the stuffed mushrooms, shrimp side up, in the pan, cover and steam over very low heat for 30 minutes.

Carefully remove the mushrooms and arrange on a warm serving dish. Pour the broth over them. Sprinkle with minced parsley.

Braised Chinese Cabbage with Chopped Prawns

HAR-YUN BOK-CHOY

蝦
仁
白
菜

1 head Chinese cabbage
1 garlic clove, minced
1 tsp. soya sauce
1 tsp. sugar
3 tbsp. rice wine or sherry

¼ cup stock or water
½ cup coarsely chopped
    cooked shrimp, hot
Seasoning powder

Wash the cabbage and cut the white stalk into small pieces, trimming away most of the leafy portion. Dry the cabbage in a clean towel.

Sauté the garlic, then add the Chinese cabbage. Cook for a minute, then add the soya sauce, sugar, and wine; season with salt and seasoning powder.

Add the stock, cover and braise 2 minutes, until the cabbage is tender, yet "crunchy." Do not overcook.

Remove the cabbage to a serving dish and sprinkle evenly with the chopped shrimp.

"Chinese like to give figurative, high-sounding and lyrical names to their dishes and that tendency is not newly developed. In ancient days, the white horse's liver and pheasant's marrow were served in state banquets in the forbidden palace under the imposing names of "dragons" liver and "phoenix" marrow of the "eight delicacies."

L. Z. YUAN, *Through a Moon Gate*

Breast of Chicken Braised with Sliced Pear

SEWT-LAY CHOW GAI

1 pair chicken breasts	Sesame oil
1 large pear, not too ripe	Salt
½ tsp. minced fresh ginger root	Pepper
1 tsp. sugar	

Skin and bone the chicken breasts and cut across the grain into slices. Core the pear and cut into thick slices.

Cook the sliced chicken slowly in sesame oil until light golden, about 2 minutes on each side. Season with salt, pepper, and the minced ginger.

Add the sliced pear, sprinkle with the sugar, then stir lightly. Cover and cook until the pear is heated through, but not too tender.

雪梨炒鷄

Braised Prawns with Powdered Aniseed

JEEN MING-HAR

2 lb. prawns
¼ cup rice wine or sherry
2 tbsp. soya sauce

2 tsp. sugar
⅔ cup stock
1 tsp. powdered aniseed

Shell, devein, and wash the prawns. Cut them in half lengthwise, then dry them in a clean towel.

Heat some oil in a pan and add the prawns, sautéing for 3 minutes. Add the wine, soya sauce, and sugar. Add the stock, cover and braise the shrimp for 3 minutes.

Remove the prawns to a warm serving dish and sprinkle the powdered aniseed evenly over them. Serve hot.

Steamed Minced Pork in Whole Eggshells

YUK-DAHN

6 eggs	1 tsp. seasoning powder
¾ cup chopped cooked pork	1 tbsp. rice wine or sherry
¾ cup chopped onion	Soya sauce
1 tsp. minced fresh ginger	Sesame oil

With a pin, carefully punch small holes in both ends of the eggs. Blow out the contents and reserve for use elsewhere. Enlarge one of the holes of each eggshell to a diameter of ⅜ inch. Wash the eggshells in hot water; drain.

Combine the pork, onion, and ginger and mince well. Add 2 tablespoons soya sauce, seasoning powder, and wine; mix well.

Stuff 4 tablespoons of this mixture carefully into each eggshell. Seal the holes by pasting tiny squares of white tissue paper over them. Place the stuffed eggshells on a dish and put in a steamer for about 30 minutes.

Serve with a sauce made by heating equal amounts of soya sauce and sesame oil.

> "All their dishes are cooked in the manner of ragouts; but they are all very different in taste, highly seasoned, and much less expensive than ours. 'The French cooks,' says F. DuHalde, 'who have refined upon everything that can awaken and excite the appetite, would be much surprised to see that the Chinese have carried the powers of invention, with respect to ragouts, much farther than they, and at a much smaller expense.'"
> ABBE GROSIER, *A General Description of China*, 1795

Steamed Omelette Rolls with Minced Duck Filling

AAP-SEE DAHN-TOONG

3 eggs
½ tsp. salt
½ cup chopped cooked duck
 (or chicken) meat
1 tsp. minced fresh ginger

1 small onion, chopped fine
⅓ cup stock, duck or chicken
2 tbsp. rice wine or sherry
½ tsp. seasoning powder

Chop the duck meat very fine. Add the minced ginger and chopped onion and mix well. Season with salt.

Beat the eggs and add the salt. Grease an 8-inch omelette pan and heat over a low fire. Remove the pan from the fire and pour in ⅓ of the egg mixture, tipping the pan to spread the egg uniformly. Return to fire and cook until the egg is set, but not too dry. Invert onto a platter, and cook the remaining egg, to yield three omelettes.

Sprinkle the omelettes with the duck meat, then roll them up into tight rolls, securing with toothpicks. Place the omelette rolls on a dish.

Place a rack in the bottom of a large pot and pour in about 2 inches water. Bring the water to boil, then turn heat down just to maintain the boiling point. Place the dish of egg rolls on the rack, cover the pot, and steam the rolls 15 minutes.

Cut the rolls into 1-inch slices and arrange on a warm serving dish.

Heat the stock, add the wine and seasoning powder, and season with salt. Pour over the egg rolls and serve hot.

Tenderloin of Beef Braised with Mushrooms & Bamboo Shoots

SEEN-SUN MO-KOO NGOW-YUK

1 lb. tenderloin of beef
2 thin slices fresh ginger root
½ cup bamboo shoots, sliced
¼ lb. fresh white mushrooms, sliced
2 tsp. soya sauce

1 tsp. sugar
1 tsp. seasoning powder
3 tbsp. rice wine or sherry
½ cup stock
Cornstarch binder

Cut the beef into small, very thin slices. Sauté the thinly sliced ginger a minute, then add the beef, bamboo shoots, and mushrooms. Sauté for 2 to 3 minutes. Add the soya sauce, sugar, seasoning powder, and wine; season with salt and pepper. Add the stock and simmer for a minute or two. Thicken the broth with cornstarch binder.

"Let salt food come first, and afterwards food of a more negative flavor. Let the heavy precede the light. Let dry dishes precede those with gravy. No flavor should dominate. If a guest eats his fill of savories, his stomach will be fatigued. Salt flavors must be relieved by bitter or hot-tasting foods, in order to restore the palate. Too much wine will make the stomach dull. Sour or sweet food will be required to rouse it again into vigor. In winter we should eat beef and mutton; in summer, dried and preserved meat. As for condiments, mustard belongs specially to summer; pepper to winter."

YUAN MEI, 1715-1797

"The greatest chef of all times in China and possibly the world over was Yieh Ya who lived around 620 B.C. His cookery book apparently was a big one and he every day served on the royal dining table a special dish. Every dish was different and no dish was repeated unless by request. Years passed and Yieh was threatened with exhaustion of his recipes. Here the most gruesome episode in his career occurred. He killed his own baby and served his flesh to the lord the next day. The lord was reported to have been greatly pleased by the new kind of meat and pressed for information as to the ingredients in the delicious dish. Yieh told the truth and was greatly rewarded for his 'loyalty.'

"While not all chefs in the imperial kitchens had to sacrifice their babies for the gastronomic satisfaction of their lords, it was dangerous although lucrative to be a member of the army of experts in the cooking department of the Forbidden City."

L. Z. YUAN, *Through a Moon Gate*

Sliced Cold Chicken Marinated in Rice Wine

J O - G A I

1 tender chicken of about 3 lb.
   Rice wine or dry sherry
¼ cup sesame oil

1 tbsp. soya sauce
   Fresh ginger root

In a garlic press, or by other means, squeeze enough slices of fresh ginger root to yield 1 teaspoon of juice.

Poach the chicken in gently simmering water, without seasoning. When tender, drain and allow to cool. Carve into thin slices as much of the meat as possible.

Place the sliced chicken in a deep bowl and pour over it about 2 cups rice wine. Allow the chicken to marinate for 2 hours, turning once or twice. Drain, then arrange the chicken slices on a serving dish.

Combine ¼ cup of the rice wine with the sesame oil, soya sauce, and ginger juice. Mix well and pour over the chicken. Serve at once.

"To the East were courtyards and gardens with many pavilions, among them "The Hall of Lovely Trees and Dark Shade," "The Autumn Pavilion," and "The Fragrance of the Green Bushes," where al fresco meals were served on hot summer days.

"The Court of Fermented Liquors in the Midst of Lotus Flowers Stirred by the Breeze" was the place where more wine was consumed than in any other part of the Flowery Kingdom. It was an exquisite spot; the lotus covered the lake, their rose-colored petals quivering in the faint breeze."

HOPE DANBY, *The Garden of Perfect Brightness*

Shrimp Cooked with Egg White, Bean Sprout Garnish

FOO-YUNG HAR-YUN

4 egg whites, beaten until frothy	½ cup chicken stock
½ tsp. cornstarch	Cornstarch binder
1 cup shelled shrimp	Pepper
¼ cup minced onion	Rice wine or sherry
⅓ lb. fresh bean sprouts	Seasoning powder

Dissolve the cornstarch in a small amount of rice wine to form a smooth paste. Add to the egg whites. Stir mixture to blend; season with salt.

Cut the shrimp into 2 or 3 pieces each. Sauté the minced onion until soft, then add the shrimp. Sauté several minutes, seasoning with salt and seasoning powder, then pour the egg-white mixture over the shrimp. Stir once just to mix, form into a small cake, and cook slowly until the egg is barely set. Remove carefully to a warm serving dish.

Heat the chicken stock and thicken with cornstarch binder. Surround the shrimp and egg with the bean sprouts, which have been parboiled in salted water until tender, yet crunchy.

Pour the chicken stock over the shrimp and sprinkle with pepper.

"The greater portion of cups, bowls, and saucers, which constitute the dinner service, consist of fine porcelain, but occasionally a few particular meats are served in silver or tutenague covers, under which is a spirit-lamp to keep them hot. The wine cups, too, are sometimes of silver gilt, and of rather elegant vase-like shapes."

J. F. DAVIS, *The Chinese*, 1864

Hard-Cooked Eggs Deep-Fried in Minced Pork Coating

YUK YERNG CHUNG-DAHN

4 eggs

1 ½ cup pork, chopped

½ tsp. salt

1 tbsp. soya sauce

2 tsp. rice wine or sherry

2 scallions, minced

1 tbsp. cornstarch

Lettuce

Hard-boil the eggs, cool and shell.

Mince the pork very fine, then add the salt, soya sauce, wine, minced scallion, and cornstarch. Mash and stir the mixture until very smooth.

Coat each egg with approx. 3 tablespoons of the pork mixture, encasing the egg evenly. Fry the eggs in deep fat until golden brown. Drain and slice each in half lengthwise.

Arrange on a bed of shredded lettuce.

"No matter what alley you enter, you are bound to see at least one house where a lantern is hung to show that tea is sold; and inside the shop you will find fresh flowers and crystal-clear rain water on the boil. These shops are always filled." WU CHING-TSU, *The Scholars*

Roast Young Chicken Stuffed with Fresh Mushrooms and Spring Onion

CHUNG-YO KUK GAI

1 roasting chicken of 4 lb.	2 tbsp. soya sauce
¼ lb. fresh mushrooms, sliced	¼ cup rice wine or sherry
1 bunch scallions	1 tbsp. sugar
3 or 4 thin slices ginger	Cornstarch binder
1 cup chicken stock	

Cut the scallions into 2-inch lengths, using both the green and white parts. Wash in hot water, drain, then dry them thoroughly in a clean towel.

Sauté the ginger slices slowly in a small amount of oil. After two minutes, add the scallions and the mushrooms and sauté them for several minutes, but do not allow the mixture to brown. Remove from the fire and allow to cool.

Dress the chicken and rub it inside and out with salt. Stuff with the mushroom-scallion mixture, truss and lard it well, then place in a roasting pan.

Mix together the chicken stock, soya sauce, wine, and sugar, and pour over the chicken. Roast the chicken in a moderate oven, basting often.

Carve and arrange on a platter together with the stuffing. Thicken ½ cup of the drippings with cornstarch binder and pour over the chicken.

Chinese Barbecued Pork

CHA-SHEW

1 lb. lean loin of pork	¼ tsp. powdered aniseed
½ tsp. salt	2 tbsp. soya sauce
¼ tsp. pepper	1 garlic clove, smashed
1 tsp. sugar	1 tbsp. rice wine or sherry
¼ tsp. cinnamon	Sesame oil, or other vegetable
¼ tsp. cloves powder	oil

Cut the pork into pieces 3 by 2 by 1 inches, the grain of the meat running lengthwise. Combine the salt, pepper, sugar, soya sauce, garlic, wine, cinnamon, aniseed, and cloves. Marinate the pork in this mixture for several hours, turning occasionally.

Preheat oven to 400°. Place the pork on a rack in a shallow roasting pan. Roast the pork 15 minutes. Turn the meat and lower the heat to 250°. Continue roasting for 25 minutes longer, basting with sesame oil.

Cut the pork across the grain into ¼-inch slices. Serve hot or cold.

"On entering the eastern main street of Peking, we found a vegetable market extemporised on each side of it; the vegetables not being on stalls, but in the vendors' baskets, as brought in from the country. They were clean and in the best of order, consisting chiefly of lettuce, cucumbers, green peas, beans, radishes, turnips, vegetable marrow, onions, and garlic."

D. F. RENNIE, *Peking and the Pekingese*

Fragrant Duck Braised with Sweet Potatoes

SHUE-JAI SHEW HERNG-AAP

1 duckling	¼ tsp. powdered aniseed
2 large sweet potatoes	1 tbsp. soya sauce
1 garlic clove, mashed	1 tsp. sugar
1 tsp. finely minced fresh ginger	1 cup chicken stock
¼ tsp. cinnamon	Cornstarch binder
¼ tsp. cloves powder	

Bone the duck and cut the meat into large pieces. Pare the sweet potatoes and cut them into ½-inch cubes. Roll them in cornstarch and fry in deep fat until golden brown. Drain well and keep warm.

Heat oil in a large skillet, and add the garlic, ginger, and duck meat. Sauté about 5 minutes, then add the sweet potatoes. Sprinkle with the cinnamon, cloves, and aniseed; add the soya sauce and sugar.

Add the stock, cover and simmer for 15 minutes, or until the duck is tender. Thicken the broth with cornstarch binder.

"Birds' nests are principally brought from Java, Sumatra, and the coasts of Malacca; they are obtained among the rocks with difficulty by men let down from their summits by a rope. They consist of a delicate sea-moss gathered from the surface of the waves by a species of swallow, and formed into nests among the precipitous cliffs. They are best when taken before they have been soiled by the bird. After having been properly cleansed, they are packed in boxes and sent to Canton, where they are often worth more than their weight in silver."

WILLIAM SPEAR, *The Oldest & the Newest Empire*, 1870

Tenderloin of Beef in Curry Sauce with Onions
KA-LEI NGOW-YUK

1 lb. tenderloin of beef
1 large onion, thinly sliced
1 tsp. sugar
½ tsp. minced fresh ginger
3 tsp. rice wine or sherry

1 tbsp. curry powder
1 tsp. seasoning powder
½ cup stock
Cornstarch binder

Cut the beef into small, very thin slices.

Sauté the onion until soft, but do not brown. Add the curry powder and minced ginger. Stir in the wine.

Add the beef and cook several minutes. Add the sugar, seasoning powder, and stock. Simmer just a minute, then thicken with cornstarch binder.

Fresh Mushrooms Braised in Oyster Sauce

HO-YO MO-KOO

1 **lb.** fresh button mushrooms	1 tsp. sugar
5 tbsp. butter	2 tsp. soya sauce
2 tbsp. oyster sauce	1 tsp. seasoning powder
2 tbsp. rice wine or sherry	

Wash the mushrooms and leave them whole. Dry them in a clean towel.

Melt the butter and sauté the mushrooms slowly until golden. Add the oyster sauce, wine, sugar, soya sauce, and seasoning powder.

Continue cooking and stirring until nearly dry. Serve hot.

"Confucius was very fastidious about his food. If his rice was not cleaned properly, or was spoiled by heat or damp, or had turned sour, he refused it. If his meat was not finely cut, or properly minced, or if it had turned a bad color or was out of season, he would not eat it, nor would he touch it unless the appropriate sauce accompanied it. The quantity of meat he ate was always in proportion to the rice, but in drinking he laid down no rules, though he carefully avoided taking too much. He would not touch meat or wine bought in the market; he always took ginger with his meals; and he did not overeat."

The Analects of Confucius

Crisp Boneless Chicken in Lemon Sauce

NING-MUNG WAN-GAI

1 tender chicken of 3 lb.	1 tsp. sugar
2 eggs, beaten	3 tbsp. fresh lemon juice
¼ cup cornstarch	Salt
½ cup flour	Pepper
1 cup rich chicken stock	Seasoning powder
¼ cup rice wine or sherry	Cornstarch binder
1 tbsp. soya sauce	Sliced lemon

Bone the chicken and cut the meat into 1-inch pieces. Combine the beaten eggs, cornstarch and flour, season with salt, pepper, and seasoning powder, and beat until smooth. Dip the pieces of chicken in this batter, then fry in deep fat until golden brown and tender. Drain and keep hot.

Heat the chicken stock, add the wine, soya sauce, sugar, and lemon juice (more or less to taste; this dish should not be too tart). Season with salt and seasoning powder, and simmer a few minutes. Thicken the broth slightly with cornstarch binder.

Add the deep-fried chicken. Stir and simmer gently for several minutes. Transfer to a serving dish and garnish with sliced lemon.

"When they had finished several cups of wine and two courses, it was time to serve soup. Now the cook was a countryman who was standing in hobnailed shoes in the courtyard enjoying the plays as he held the tray with six bowls of soup. The servant had taken four of his bowls away, and there were still two left. But at the sight of an actor singing and posturing as a singsong girl, the cook was so carried away that he forgot all else, thought all the soup had been served and let the tray down to pour off any slops. The two bowls were smashed, and all the soup spilt. Losing his head, the cook bent down to mop up the soup, but two dogs got there before him and started licking it up. Furious, the cook kicked with all his might at the dogs. In his haste, however, he missed the dogs and one of his hobnailed shoes flew off ten feet into the air.

"Now Chen Ho-Fu happened to be sitting at the first table on the left, where two plates of food had been served: One plate of pork dumplings, the other of dumplings stuffed with goose fat and sugar. These dumplings were steaming hot and there was another bowl of soup before him. He was just raising his chopsticks to his mouth when something black hurtled from behind the table to smash the two plates of sweetmeats. And as Chen Ho-Fu jumped up in a fright, he caught the bowl of soup with his sleeve and overturned it, so that it slopped all over the table. Everybody present was taken aback."

WU CHING-TSU, *The Scholars*

Braised Stuffed Cucumbers

YERNG WONG-GWA

6 small cucumbers
1 egg, beaten
½ tsp. cornstarch
1 tsp. soya sauce
¾ cup stock

1 cup chopped cooked pork (or
  shrimp or chicken)
3 tbsp. rice wine or sherry
  Cornstarch binder

Pare the cucumbers and cut them in half lengthwise. Scoop out the center, leaving a smooth cavity.

Mince the pork well and mix in the beaten egg and cornstarch. Season with salt. Fill each cucumber with 4 teaspoons of this mixture.

Fry the stuffed cucumbers, filling side down, until light golden brown. Turn them over, and add the soya sauce, stock, and wine. Cover the pan and braise the cucumbers until tender, about 20 minutes.

Remove the cucumbers to a serving dish. Thicken the broth with cornstarch binder and pour over the cucumbers.

"Then tea in beautiful cups with silver saucers was offered. The saucers were not round, but oval, pointed at each end. Various kinds of sweetmeats were given with the tea, the finest being crystallized Siberian crabs.

"A very toothsome sauce was poured from an exquisite little china teapot into a porcelain spoon that was laid on a saucer for each.

"The napkins were beautiful squares of silk of a pale olive green, lined with pink satin. One corner of each was folded down, and a silk cord sewed on to serve as a button-latch."

ISABELLE WILLIAMSON, *Old Highways in China*, 1883

Fish Croquettes over Braised Chinese Cabbage

BOK-CHOY PA YEW-WAN

2 lb. fillet of fish
1/4 cup water
1 tsp. salt
1/2 tsp. pepper
1/2 tsp. sugar
1/4 cup rice wine or sherry

1 tsp. soya sauce
3 tbsp. flour
  Fresh ginger root
1 head Chinese cabbage, sliced
1/3 cup stock
  Cornstarch binder

Mince the fish fine, then place in a large bowl. Add the water, salt, pepper, sugar, and flour, and mix well. Stir and mash with a spoon until the mixture is smooth.

Form the mixture into small balls and fry them in oil until golden brown. Drain and sprinkle with salt. Keep them warm.

Heat a small amount of oil in a pan and add a few thin slices of fresh ginger root. After a minute, add the sliced cabbage and sauté until it is tender, yet "crunchy." Season with salt. Remove the cabbage to a warm serving dish.

Heat the stock and add the wine and soya sauce. Season with salt, pepper, and a pinch of sugar. Simmer a minute, then thicken the sauce with cornstarch binder.

Arrange the fish croquettes over the cooked cabbage, and pour the sauce over all.

Poached Shrimp with Spiced Egg Sauce

POON MING-HAR

1 lb. fresh shrimp
3 egg yolks
¼ cup butter
¼ cup white vinegar

1 tsp. powdered English mustard
Rice wine or sherry
Shredded lettuce

Shell, devein, and wash the shrimp. Bring a pot of water to boil, adding salt and white wine. Add the shrimp and let them simmer until pink, about 4 minutes. Do not overcook. Drain the shrimp and cut them into 2 or 3 pieces each, depending on their size. Keep warm.

Beat the egg yolks and add the vinegar and mustard powder, and season with salt. Melt the butter in a pan, then add the egg mixture. Mix well over a low fire until thickened. The eggs should not congeal completely.

Arrange the shrimp on shredded lettuce and pour the egg sauce over. Serve at once.

"Presently the table was strewn with flowers, pretty baskets filled with the same, and plates which contained a vast variety of delicious sweetmeats as well as cakes, of which the forms were as ingenious as they were varied. By the side of the yellow plantain was seen the litchi, of which the strong, rough, and bright crimson skin defends a stone enveloped in a whitish pulp, which for its fine aromatic taste is superior to most of the tropical fruits."

J. F. DAVIS, *The Chinese*, 1864

Duckling Braised with Chestnuts & Sliced Pear

LEWT-JEE SEWT-LAY AAP

½ lb. chestnuts
1 duckling, about 3 lb.
2 tbsp. soya sauce
2 tbsp. rice wine or sherry

1 tsp. fresh ginger root, minced
1 cup stock
1 large pear, peeled and sliced
1 tsp. sugar

Clean and disjoint the duckling, then chop it through the bones into 2-inch pieces. Brown the duck in oil, then pour off as much fat as possible.

Add the soya sauce, rice wine, and ginger to the duck. Season with salt, then pour the stock over. Cover and simmer for 30 minutes.

Add the chestnuts, which have been parboiled for 15 minutes and shelled, then cook for 10 minutes. Add the sliced pear, sprinkle with the sugar, stir gently, and allow to cook for 5 minutes longer, until the pear is heated through, but not too tender.

"The bank was lined with taverns hung with fat mutton, while the plates on the counters were heaped with steaming trotters, sea slugs, duck preserved in wine, and fresh water fish. Meat dumplings boiled in the cauldrons and enormous rolls of bread filled the steamers."
WU CHING-TSU, *The Scholars*

栗子雪梨鴨

34

Ham Rolls with Chicken & Walnut Filling, Sauce with Mushrooms & Bamboo Shoots

FOH-TOY GWEN

8 thin slices of lean cooked ham	1 tsp. cornstarch
1 cup minced cooked chicken meat	1/4 lb. fresh white button mushrooms
1/4 cup finely chopped walnuts	1 medium onion, sliced thin
1 tbsp. sesame oil	1 tsp. sugar
1 tsp. seasoning powder	2 tsp. catsup
1/2 cup bamboo shoots, fresh or canned	1/4 cup rice wine or sherry
	1/2 cup stock

Combine the minced chicken, walnuts, sesame oil, seasoning powder, and cornstarch. Mix well until smooth, then season with salt and pepper.

Divide and spread this mixture evenly over the eight slices of ham. Roll up each slice to form a tight roll. Secure the rolls with toothpicks. Fry them in 1 inch of hot fat for 3 to 5 minutes, until they are a rich reddish-brown, but not crisp. Drain and remove the toothpicks. Keep warm.

Sauté the sliced bamboo shoots, mushrooms, and onion in a minimum amount of oil, until they are barely tender. Add the sugar, catsup, stock and wine. Season with salt. Allow to simmer a minute or two; do not allow the vegetables to become too tender. Thicken the broth with corn-starch binder.

Arrange the ham rolls on a serving dish and pour the vegetable sauce over them.

35

"The best meat dish is made from the lips of the orangutang, from the tails of young swallows, the marrow of buffaloes and elephants. To the west of the wandering dunes of the red mountains there are phoenix eggs which the people of Yu eat. The best fish is the turbot from the Tsung T'ung Lake and the sardines of the Western Sea. In the Necta Springs there lives a fish called Scarlet Turtle, it has six legs and pearls as if of green jade. In the deep sea there is a fish called the flying fish. It looks like a carp and has wings with which it can rise above the water.

"Among vegetables, the best are the seaweeds which grow near Mt. Kunlun, they are the fruit of the tree of life. On the shores of the South Pole there is a vegetable called the tree of recognition, its color is that of green jade. The best parsley comes from the Hua mountains and the best celery from the Yun Mong Lake. In Ts'in Yuan there is an herb which is called Earth Blossom.

"Among the spices the best are ginger from Yangpu, cinnamon from Chao Yao, mushrooms from Tuolo, sauce made from eels and pike, and salt from Tahsia.

"Among fruits, the best are the ones from the apple tree. North of the Chao range there are all kinds of fruit eaten by the gods. In the South there are sweet oranges, mandarins and pomelos from the River Wan. The fastest horses are required to fetch them."

I YIN, 2000 B.C.

Tenderloin of Beef Braised in Oyster Sauce

HO-YO NGOW-YUK

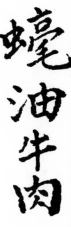

1 lb. tenderloin of beef	1 tsp. seasoning powder
1 garlic clove, minced	3 tbsp. rice wine or sherry
1 small onion, sliced thin	1 tsp. fresh ginger root, minced
1 tbsp. soya sauce	½ cup stock
2 tbsp. Chinese oyster sauce	Cornstarch binder
1 tsp. sugar	

Cut the beef into small, very thin slices.

Sauté the garlic and onion a minute or two. Add the beef and cook 2 minutes. Add the soya sauce, oyster sauce, sugar, seasoning powder, wine, and ginger; season with salt and pepper. Stir well.

Add the stock and simmer for just a minute. Thicken the broth with cornstarch binder.

> "Do not roll the rice into a ball; do not bolt down the various dishes; do not swill down the soup.
> "Do not make a noise (in eating); do not throw bones to the dogs; do not crunch bones with the teeth; do not put back fish you have begun to eat; do not snatch.
> "Do not spread out the rice (to cool); do not gulp down soup with vegetables in it, nor add condiments to it; if the guest add condiments the host will apologize for not having had the soup made better.
> "Do not pick the teeth; do not bolt roast meat in large pieces."
> From the *Book of Rites*

Breast of Lamb in Casserole with Ground Rice

FUN JING YERNG-YUK

2 lb. lean breast of lamb, or
    shoulder
½ cup "Cream of Rice" dry
    granulated rice
2 tbsp. sugar

4 tbsp. soya sauce
2 tbsp. A-1 steak sauce
2 tbsp. rice wine or sherry
3 cups stock

Cut the lamb into 1-inch cubes. Place the lamb in a small casserole and add the dry ground rice, sugar, soya sauce, A-1 sauce, wine, and stock.

Mix well and cover the casserole. Place in a moderate oven and bake for about 1½ hours, until the meat is tender and all the broth is absorbed. Add additional stock during cooking if necessary to prevent scorching.

Spareribs Barbecued with Fragrant Spices

NG-HERNG PAI-GOOT

2 lb. lean pork spareribs	4 tbsp. soya sauce
2 tbsp. rice wine or sherry	½ tsp. powdered aniseed
1 tbsp. sugar	½ tsp. cloves powder
2 garlic cloves, mashed	1 tsp. salt
½ tsp. cinnamon	Hot English mustard

Do not cut the ribs apart. Combine the soya sauce, wine, sugar, garlic, cinnamon, aniseed, cloves, and salt. Marinate the spareribs in this mixture for 2 hours.

Roast the spareribs on a rack in a 325° oven for one hour, basting. Chop the ribs apart and serve with hot mustard.

Steamed Minced Chicken

JING BOK-FA GAI

2 cups chopped raw chicken meat
½ tsp. salt
1 tsp. peanut oil
2 tsp. cornstarch
¼ cup minced ham

½ cup chicken stock
1 tsp. seasoning powder
Soya sauce
Cornstarch binder

Mince the chicken meat very fine, then add 1 tablespoon soya sauce, salt, peanut oil, and cornstarch. Mix thoroughly, then place on a dish and form into a large, flat patty. Sprinkle with the minced ham.

Place the dish on a rack in a large pot containing 3 inches boiling water. Cover and steam for 20 minutes, or until chicken is cooked.

Meanwhile, heat the chicken stock and add the seasoning powder together with 1 tablespoon soya sauce. Thicken with cornstarch binder, then pour over the steamed chicken.

"Talking today of the talent which the Chinese have for cookery, Mr. Thorburn mentioned a curious and cruel receipt for cooking turtles which appears in one of their cookery books. The turtle is placed in a vessel of water on the fire, with a lid over it having an aperture of sufficient size, and so arranged that the turtle can just get his head out, and within the reach of a highly-spiced wine. As the temperature of the water increases, so does his thirst, and he gradually goes on drinking the seasoned fluid until the heat kills him, by which time his whole system has become impregnated with the vino-aromatic seasoning, and a flavor described as delicious, is imparted to the flesh."

D. F. RENNIE, *Peking and the Pekingese*

Prawns Fried in Wine Batter

SHUI-CHING HAR-YUN

1 lb. fresh prawns	¾ tsp. salt
2 eggs	1 tsp. seasoning powder
¼ cup cornstarch	⅓ cup rice wine or sherry
½ cup flour	Lettuce

Shell, devein, and wash the prawns. Slice them in half lengthwise. Beat the eggs and add the cornstarch, flour, salt, and seasoning powder. Mix until smooth.

Dip the prawns into the batter and fry them in deep fat until golden brown. Drain.

Pour the wine into a large skillet and heat to boiling. Add the fried prawns and simmer until the wine is absorbed, turning the shrimp once.

Serve them on a bed of shredded lettuce.

"Soon after being seated, the attendants invariably enter with porcelain cups furnished with covers, in each of which, on removing the little saucer by which it is surmounted, appears a small quantity of fine tealeaves. Though the infusion is generally made in the cup, they occasionally use teapots of antique and tasteful shapes, which are not infrequently made of tutenague externally, covering earthenware on the inside."

J. F. DAVIS, *The Chinese*, 1864

Braised Tenderloin of Pork over Bean Sprouts, Egg Garnish

FUNG-WONG CHOW SAM-SEE

   1 egg
½ lb. tenderloin of pork
¼ cup minced onion
   3 small dried mushrooms,
       soaked 15 minutes
   2 tsp. soya sauce

   1 tsp. sugar
½ tsp. seasoning powder
   3 tbsp. rice wine or sherry
½ cup stock
⅓ lb. bean sprouts

Beat the egg and season with salt. Pour into a hot greased omelette pan and tip to distribute evenly. Cook over low heat until set, but not too dry. Invert onto a platter and cut into narrow strips when cool.

Cut the pork into thin slices and sauté together with the minced onion and the sliced mushrooms. Add the soya sauce, sugar, seasoning powder, and wine. Season with salt, then add the stock. Cover and simmer.

Meanwhile, sauté the bean sprouts, seasoning with salt and seasoning powder, until tender, yet crunchy. Arrange on a warm serving platter.

When the pork is cooked and the liquid is considerably reduced, dress the mixture over the bean sprouts.

Garnish with the omelette strips.

Deep-Fried Marinated Chicken

LAU JA-GAI

1 young chicken of 3 lb.	1 tsp. sugar
½ cup soya sauce	1 tsp. fresh ginger, chopped fine
¼ cup rice wine or sherry	Sifted cornstarch

Bone the chicken and cut the meat into 1-inch pieces.

Combine the soya sauce, wine, sugar, and ginger. Add the chicken meat, stirring to coat it well, and allow it to marinate for 30 minutes or longer. Drain the chicken well and save the marinade. Dry the chicken as much as possible by patting it with paper towels.

Fry the chicken in deep fat until light golden. Drain well and return to the marinade while hot, stirring and allowing to stand for 15 minutes.

Drain the chicken, then dust it lightly with the sifted cornstarch. Refry the chicken pieces in deep fat until crisp and golden brown.

"We sat down to a most excellent dinner, wholly prepared in the Chinese style, consisting of a variety of made dishes very neatly dressed, and served in porcelain bowls. The best soup I ever tasted in any part of the world was made here from an extract of beef, seasoned with a preparation of soya and other ingredients. Their vermicelli is excellent, and all their pastry is usually as white as snow."

HOPE DANBY, *The Garden of Perfect Brightness*

Beef Smoked with Fragrant Spices

FUN NGOW-YUK

½ lb. tenderloin of beef	½ cup dark brown sugar
3 tbsp. soya sauce	2 tsp. cinnamon
3 tbsp. rice wine or sherry	2 tsp. powdered aniseed
1 tsp. sugar	2 tsp. cloves powder

Cut the beef into small, very thin slices. Place the meat in a shallow pan and add the soya sauce, wine, and sugar. Allow to marinate for one hour.

Place the pan over medium heat, turning the meat until it is tender.

Place a sheet of heavy aluminum foil in the bottom of a large cast-iron pot. Combine the brown sugar, cinnamon, aniseed, and cloves and spread over the foil. Support a wire rack inside the pot, about 2 inches above the spice mixture.

Arrange the slices of beef on the rack and cover the pot tightly. Place the pot over a low fire and allow to smoke for about 10 minutes.

Serve the beef hot or cold. Be sure to turn on the fan or open the windows for this preparation; the smoking pot can be placed on hot coals in the outdoor barbecue.

> "The nun poured tea in a cup made in the Ch'eng Hua period (A.D. 1665-88) and presented it to the Matriarch on a tray of carved laquer. The Matriarch asked her what water was used, and the nun answered that it was rain water saved from the year before. The Matriarch drank half the cup and gave the rest to Liu Lao-Lao, saying, "You taste this tea, too." She did so. When asked how she liked it, she said it was too light."
>
> From the *Dream of The Red Chamber*

Boneless Duck Steamed in Whole Watermelon with Button Mushrooms

JING SAI-GWA AAP

1 medium watermelon	¾ cup rice wine or sherry
1 tender duckling	3 tsp. seasoning powder
1 cup cubed ham	2 tsp. soya sauce
6 dried black mushrooms	1 tsp. aniseed
¼ lb. white button mushrooms	Duck or chicken stock

Lay the melon on its side and cut a 6-inch hole out of the side. Save this piece as a "lid." Scoop out and discard the seedy portion of the melon.

Bone the duck and cut the meat into small pieces. Soak the dried mushrooms in hot water 15 minutes, then slice thin.

Mix together the duck meat, ham, black mushrooms, button mushrooms, and wine, seasoning powder, soya sauce, and aniseed. Stuff this mixture into the watermelon. Add duck or chicken stock until the melon is full. Replace the melon lid.

Place a rack in a large roasting pan, pouring 2 inches of water into the bottom. Support the melon on the rack, so that the hole remains upright.

Cover the pan tightly. Place on two stove burners, and steam for 4 to 5 hours, until the melon is very tender and the duck cooked. Replenish the water in the pan when necessary during the cooking period.

To serve, carefully lift out the melon and transfer to an attractive supporting bowl. Remove the "lid" of the melon and ladle the contents into individual bowls at the table.

"The brothers invited guests and hired two big boats; the cooks prepared a feast; and they filled another boat with attendants; and yet another with musicians and singers. This was the middle of the fourth month when the weather was clear and warm; so all the guests were wearing summer clothes and carrying fans.

"The cabin windows on both sides were opened, so that they could hear music from the small boats as they drifted towards the lake. And presently a feast was spread and a dozen servants in wide gowns and tall caps poured wine and served the dishes. It goes without saying that the food was rare, the wine and tea were fragrant, and they drank till the moon was up. Then fifty or sixty lanterns were lit on the small boats and were reflected with the moonlight in the water, making it as bright as day.

"The music sounded even more clearly in the stillness, its strains echoing for miles around, so that the watchers on shore stared at the revellers as if they were immortals, and none but envied them.

"Thus they boated all night."

WU CHING-TSU, *The Scholars*

Curried Tenderloin of Pork Braised with Sweet Potatoes

KA-LEI SHUE-JAI YUK

嘅喱薯仔肉

2 large sweet potatoes
1 lb. tenderloin of pork
½ tsp. minced ginger
1 small onion, thinly sliced

1 tbsp. soya sauce
1 tbsp. curry powder
1 cup stock
Cornstarch binder

Pare the sweet potatoes and cut them into slices ½ inch thick. Fry them in deep fat for about 5 minutes, until light golden brown. Drain.

Cut the pork into ½-inch cubes. Sauté them with the ginger and onion until browned. Add the soya sauce and season with salt and pepper. Add the curry powder and the stock. Stir well, then add the deep-fried sweet potatoes.

Cover and stew slowly until the pork is cooked. Thicken the sauce with cornstarch binder, if necessary.

"Peking has been described as the 'Mecca of all gourmets of the Chinese Empire,' and sumptuous banquets were frequently given in the Yuan Ming Yuan. Whenever an important personage, considered worthy of the Emperor's hospitality, visited the capital, he was invited to a feast. The meals were endless affairs, and served on plates of massy gold, silver, pewter, and delicately painted porcelain; the dishes ran into hundreds and were seasoned with the Five Flavors, the sweet, sour, salty, spicy, and bitter. Epicurean delicacies were received from thousands of miles away, many of them packed in ice and salt to preserve them."

HOPE DANBY, *The Garden of Perfect Brightness*

Sliced Cold Chicken with Honey-Oyster Sauce

MUT WAN-GAI

1 tender chicken of 3 lb.
½ cup honey
¼ cup Chinese oyster sauce
1 tsp. salt

1 tsp. seasoning powder
¼ cup scallion, chopped fine
1 tbsp. fresh ginger root, minced

Poach the chicken in gently simmering water, without seasoning. When tender, drain and allow to cool. Then carve into thin slices as much of the meat as possible. Arrange the slices on a serving dish.

Combine the honey, oyster sauce, salt, and seasoning powder. Mix well, then pour over the chicken. Sprinkle with the chopped scallion and minced ginger.

"Don't eat with your ears! By this I mean do not aim at having extraordinary out-of-the-way foods, just to astonish your guests. Bean curd, if good, is actually nicer than bird's nest. And better than sea-slugs (beche-de-mer), if not first rate, is a dish of bamboo-shoots.

"Don't eat with your eyes! By this I mean do not cover the table with innumerable dishes and multiply courses indefinitely. For this is to eat with the eyes; not with the mouth."

YUAN MEI, 1715-1797

Prawns Braised with Sliced Bamboo Shoots

SEEN-SUN HAR-YUN

1 lb. fresh prawns
1 cup sliced bamboo shoots
¼ cup rice wine or sherry
¼ cup stock
2 tbsp. ham, chopped fine

1 tsp. soya sauce
½ tsp. sugar
White vinegar
Sesame oil

Shell, devein, and wash the prawns. Cut them in half lengthwise and sprinkle with salt.

Heat a small amount of oil and sauté the bamboo shoots several minutes. Add the soya sauce, sugar, and wine. Add the prawns and then the stock. Cover and simmer until the prawns are just tender.

Transfer the mixture to a warm serving dish and sprinkle with the chopped ham. Then sprinkle a few drops each of distilled vinegar and sesame oil over the dish.

"We drank the wine in little gilt cups, having the shape of an antique vase, with two handles of perfect workmanship, and kept constantly filled by attendants holding large silver vessels like coffee pots."

J. F. DAVIS, *The Chinese*, 1864

Tenderloin of Pork Braised with Green Olives

WAN-BO YUK

1 lb. tenderloin of pork
1 tbsp. soya sauce
1 tsp. seasoning powder

¼ cup rice wine or sherry
10 green olives
¼ cup stock

Cut the pork into ½-inch cubes and sauté until lightly browned. Add the soya sauce, seasoning powder, and wine; season with salt.

Cover and braise until the pork is nearly done. Add the green olives, whose skins have been scored with a knife, and the stock. Cover and simmer 10 minutes longer.

Soup with White Vegetables

BOK-YUK TONG

½ cup bean sprouts
1 cake bean curd
½ cup bamboo shoots, sliced

½ cup fresh white button
mushrooms
3 cups rich chicken stock

Wash and drain the bean sprouts. Cut the bean curd into small cubes. Slice the mushrooms very thin.

Bring the chicken stock to boil, add the bean sprouts, bean curd, button mushrooms, and bamboo shoots. Simmer the soup for 3 minutes, then season with salt.

Duckling Braised with Sliced Young Ginger

GERNG-NGA AAP-PEEN

½ cup fresh new ginger root,
    peeled and sliced
1 duckling of 3 lb.
2 egg whites, beaten until frothy
    Cornstarch

1 green bell pepper, cut into
    strips
2 tbsp. rice wine or sherry
    Sugar
    Rice vinegar or distilled vinegar
1 cup stock

Sprinkle the sliced ginger with 1 tablespoon salt, mix and allow to stand 5 minutes. Wash off the salt and drain the ginger. Place in a dish and mix with 1 tablespoon sugar and 3 tablespoons distilled vinegar. Let stand 2 hours, then drain well.

Clean and disjoint the duckling, then chop it through the bones into 2-inch pieces. Dip each piece in the egg white, then dust with the sifted cornstarch. Fry the duck in deep fat until golden brown. Drain.

Sauté the ginger together with the green pepper for several minutes. Add the duckling, rice wine, 1 teaspoon sugar, and 2 teaspoons vinegar. Season with salt.

Add the stock, cover and simmer slowly for 15 minutes, or until the duck is tender.

> "Upon a brilliantly varnished table was placed a magnificent collation of pastry and fruit, amidst which rose conspicuously an enormous water-melon, the thick black skin of which had been carved in fanciful designs by a Chinese engraver. By the side of the table was a pedestal, supporting an antique porcelain jar full of lemonade."
>
> M. HUC, *Journey through the Chinese Empire*, 1854

Deep-Fried Fillet of Fish Stuffed with Pork, Garnished with Hard-Cooked Eggs

HOONG-CHUNG-DAHN YEW

4 eggs, hard-cooked
8 small fillets of any white fish
1 cup stock
1 tsp. soya sauce
¼ cup onion, chopped

1 cup cooked pork, minced well
1 tsp. ginger, minced
Sugar
Rice wine or sherry
Cornstarch binder

Carefully shell the eggs and dry them well with a towel. Fry them in deep fat until golden brown. Drain and keep hot.

Combine the pork with 1 teaspoon sugar and 3 tablespoons rice wine or sherry. Mix until smooth. Spread 2 tablespoons of this mixture over each fillet. Fold the fillets over once or twice and secure them with toothpicks.

Fry the stuffed fillets in deep fat until light golden brown. Drain and keep warm.

Heat the stock, add 2 tablespoons rice wine, ½ teaspoon sugar, the soya sauce, onion, and ginger. Bring to boil and simmer a minute, then thicken slightly with cornstarch binder.

Arrange the fish on a warm serving dish. Slice the eggs in half lengthwise and arrange them around the fish. Pour the gravy over all.

"Apart from foods which are poisonous in themselves, there are many which should not be eaten together as they do not harmonize and are apt to cause great discomfort and inconvenience. Horse flesh, for example, should not be accompanied by ginger; neither should hare. Pork and beef, or pork and sheep-liver are equally unsuited to be eaten together."

From the *Imperial Cookery Book of the Mongol Dynasty*

Tenderloin of Pork Braised with Bamboo Shoots & Green Peppers, Sweet-Sour Sauce

GOO-LAO YUK

1 lb. pork tenderloin	½ cup distilled vinegar
2 tbsp. rice wine or sherry	2 tsp. soya sauce
Cornstarch	1 cup bamboo shoots, sliced
1 tsp. fresh ginger root, minced	1 large green bell pepper,
½ cup chopped onion	cut into strips
1 cup tomato sauce	Soya sauce
½ cup water	Cornstarch binder
½ cup sugar	

Sauté the ginger and onion for a moment, then add the tomato sauce and water. Cover and simmer slowly for 20 minutes. Stir in the sugar, vinegar, and 2 teaspoons soya sauce. Cook for 2 minutes, then strain the sauce.

Cut the pork into 1-inch cubes. Combine 2 tablespoons soya sauce and rice wine, and marinate the pork in this mixture for 15 minutes, stirring once or twice. Drain the pork well. Dust the cubes with cornstarch and fry them in deep fat until golden brown and thoroughly cooked. Drain and keep warm.

Bring the sweet-sour sauce to a boil and add the bamboo shoots and green pepper. Cook for 2 minutes, then thicken the sauce slightly with cornstarch binder. Add the deep-fried pork and heat through.

"During one of his tours, the emperor Chien Lung (1736-1789) found a non-greasy, delicious appetizing dish in a small city near Hangchow. Upon his inquiry, the magistrate informed the ruler that the name of the dish was "Red-Beaked Green Parrot with Gold Trimmed Jade Cake." In reality, the dish was a cheap affair, the main ingredients being spinach (with the crimson roots) and fried bean curd. The magistrate had to give a figurative name for fear that the cheapness of the dish would arouse imperial resentment.

"When the emperor returned to Peking, he recalled the delicious dish and sent an order to his imperial kitchen for an order of the so-called dish. His army of chefs was puzzled. The head chef finally bought a parrot from the bird market, slaughtered it, and served it with a piece of valuable jade. His matter-of-fact interpretation of the name of the dish incurred the emperor's wrath. The chef was punished with decapitation for spoiling the imperial appetite."

L. Z. YUAN, *Through a Moon Gate*

Boneless Chicken in Tomato Sauce with Fresh Garden Peas

FAHN-KAIR GAI-KOW

1 young chicken of 3 lb.
2 egg whites, beaten until frothy
Cornstarch
1 cup green peas, fresh or frozen
2 tbsp. rice wine or sherry
1 tsp. sugar
1 tsp. salt
¼ cup tomato catsup
¾ cup chicken stock

Clean and disjoint the chicken, then chop it through the bones into 2-inch pieces. Dip each piece in the egg white, then dust with cornstarch. Fry the chicken in deep fat until golden brown. Drain.

Sauté the green peas for just a moment, then add the wine, sugar, salt, and catsup. Stir in the chicken stock, then add the deep-fried chicken. Simmer covered for 15 minutes, or until the chicken is tender.

"Sitting in the small boat with their luggage, the two brothers looked at the mulberry trees which grew so thickly along either bank and the wild fowl which were crying as they flew. They had gone three or four hundred yards only when they came to a small creek and saw boats gliding out selling water chestnuts and lotus roots."

WU CHING-TSU, *The Scholars*

Crisp Boneless Chicken, Curry Sauce

KA-LEI WAN-GAI

1 chicken of 3 lb.
2 eggs, beaten
¼ cup cornstarch
½ cup flour
Salt
Pepper

Seasoning powder
¼ lb. butter
2 tsp. curry powder
¼ cup rice wine or sherry
Lettuce

嚹喱軟鷄

Bone the chicken and cut the meat into 1-inch pieces.

Combine the beaten eggs, cornstarch, and flour, season with salt, pepper, and seasoning powder, and beat until smooth. Dip the pieces of chicken in this batter, then fry in deep fat until golden brown and tender. Drain well.

Melt the butter slowly and stir in the curry powder (more or less to taste) until smooth. Thin this sauce with the wine, stirring all the while.

Arrange the cooked chicken over shredded lettuce, and sprinkle the curry sauce over it. Serve at once.

"Cookery is like matrimony—two things served together must match."

YUAN MEI, 1715-1797

Sea Scallops Steamed with Ham

FOH-TOY JING GON-CHEW

1 lb. sea scallops	1 tsp. fresh ginger root, minced
1 cup rice wine or sherry	1 cup Virginia ham, shredded
1/4 cup onion, chopped fine	1 tsp. sugar

Wash the scallops, then marinate them in the rice wine for two hours. Drain them, then cut each scallop into four slices.

Arrange the slices on a dish. Sprinkle the minced ginger and chopped onion over them, then sprinkle with salt.

Arrange the shredded ham evenly over the scallops, then sprinkle with the sugar. Place the dish in a steamer for 10 to 15 minutes, or until the scallops are tender.

"Let tea remain in the cup as long as the vapor rises in a cloud, and leaves only a thin mist floating over the surface. At your ease, drink this precious liquor, which will chase away the five causes of trouble. We can taste and feel, but not describe, the state of repose produced by such tea."

THE EMPEROR CHIEN LUNG, from *An Ode on Tea*

Chicken & Shrimp Baked in Meringue

BOK-SEWT GAI

3 pairs chicken breasts	¼ cup parsley, finely chopped
½ lb. fresh shrimp	Rice wine or sherry
¼ cup finely minced ham	Seasoning powder
3 egg whites	Cornstarch

Shell and clean the shrimp. Dry thoroughly, then chop fine. Season with salt, seasoning powder, and a dash of wine; mix well until smooth.

Bone and skin the chicken breasts and cut the meat into fine strips. Mix the chicken in a bowl with ¼ cup wine, and season with salt and seasoning powder. Allow to marinate a few minutes.

Butter an 8-inch oven-proof dish lightly; sprinkle with cornstarch, then shake off the excess. Lay the chicken strips, one by one, in the dish, criss-crossing and forming a solid bed of chicken meat. Sprinkle lightly with cornstarch.

Press the shrimp mixture evenly over the chicken. Place the dish in a moderate oven for 20 minutes.

Meanwhile, beat the egg whites until stiff. Do not season in any way. Spread the egg whites over the chicken-shrimp dish. Sprinkle the meringue with the minced ham and chopped parsley, forming small flower patterns.

Return the dish to the oven for 10 minutes, or until the meringue is lightly browned.

Cut into 2-inch squares and serve hot.

Spareribs Braised in Tomato Sauce

KAIR-JUP JEEN JEW-PAI

2 lb. lean pork spareribs	2 eggs, beaten
5 tbsp. soya sauce	Fine cracker crumbs
2 tbsp. rice wine or sherry	1 large onion, sliced thin
1 tsp. seasoning powder	2 tsp. sugar
¼ cup tomato catsup	1 cup stock

Cut the spareribs in 2-inch lengths. Combine 4 tablespoons soya sauce, wine, and seasoning powder. Marinate the spareribs in this mixture for one hour, turning occasionally.

Dip the spareribs in beaten egg, then roll in fine cracker crumbs. Fry the ribs in deep fat, a few at a time, until golden brown. Drain and keep warm.

Sauté the sliced onion until soft, but do not brown. Add the 1 tablespoon soya sauce, sugar, and catsup. Add the stock and simmer a moment.

Add the spareribs and braise until they are tender.

"To know right from wrong, a man must be sober. And only a sober man can distinguish good flavors from bad. It has been well said that words are inadequate to describe the various shades of taste. How much less then must a stuttering sot be able to appreciate them!"

YUAN MEI, 1715-1797

Chicken Livers in Oyster Sauce with Mushrooms

HO-YO JUN-GON

1 lb. chicken livers	1 tbsp. soya sauce
¼ lb. mushrooms, sliced	1 tsp. seasoning powder
1 medium onion, sliced very thin	½ tsp. sugar
1 cup chicken stock	Butter
1 tbsp. rice wine or sherry	Cornstarch binder
2 tbsp. Chinese oyster sauce	

Sauté the mushrooms and onion in butter until tender, but not browned. Set aside and keep warm.

Wash the chicken livers in hot water and dry them in a clean towel. Cut them in half. Melt 3 tablespoons butter in a skillet; add the chicken livers and sauté 5 minutes.

Add the mushroom-and-onion mixture. Add the stock, wine, oyster sauce, soya sauce, seasoning powder, and sugar. Stir, then simmer for 5 minutes.

Thicken the sauce slightly with cornstarch binder.

"The greater part of the inhabitants of Cathay drink a sort of wine made from rice mixed with a variety of spices and drugs. This beverage is so good and well flavored that they could not wish for better. It is clear, bright and pleasant to the taste, and being made very hot, has the quality of inebriating sooner than any other."

MARCO POLO

Tenderloin of Pork Braised with Orange Peel

GWAW-PAY YUK

1 lb. tenderloin of pork
1 tsp. minced fresh ginger
¼ cup chopped onion
2 tbsp. orange rind, chopped fine
1 tbsp. soya sauce

¼ cup rice wine or sherry
1 tsp. sugar
1 cup stock
Cayenne pepper

Cut the pork into ½-inch cubes. Heat a small amount of oil in a pan and add the ginger and onion. Add the pork cubes and sauté until the pork is lightly browned.

Add the chopped orange peel, soya sauce, wine, and sugar. Season with salt and cayenne pepper. Add the stock, cover and braise slowly until the pork is done, about 30 minutes.

Deep-Fried Fillet of Fish in Batter with Sesame Seeds

JEE-MAH YEW-PAI

芝麻魚排

8 small fillets of any white fish
1 cup rice wine or sherry
3 tbsp. minced onion
1 tsp. minced ginger
1 tsp. salt
1 tbsp. sugar
¼ cup cornstarch
½ cup flour
2 eggs, beaten
White sesame seeds

Prepare a marinade of the wine, onion, ginger, salt, and sugar. Place the fillets in this mixture and allow to marinate 15 minutes.

Combine the cornstarch with the flour and eggs and beat until smooth. Dip the drained fillets into this batter, then roll them in white sesame seeds. Fry in 1 inch of oil until golden brown.

"The empty sides of the table where no one sat were hung with scarlet drapery, beautifully worked in embroidery of gold and different colored silks. On the front edge of each table were placed the finest fruits in little baskets, with beautiful flowers stuck between them. Besides these the whole table was covered with little cups and plates, which were ranged with great precision, and contained fruits, preserves, confectionery, slices of bread and butter, with small birds cold, and hundreds of other things. An extraordinary degree of art had been expended in the arrangement of those articles; amongst the rest were whole rows of little plates filled with elegantly-raised three- and four-cornered pyramids, composed of little bits of pheasant, larded geese, sausages, and so forth. Here stood plates of small oranges; there, preserved plums; and here again, almonds. Various little seeds of different colors were served upon shallow saucers, so arranged, however, that each color occupied a particular field. There were quince seeds, of very delicate flavor, chick peas, chestnuts and hazel nuts; also grapes and preserved ginger, citron, and lemon.

"By way of cover, three small cups are placed before each seat; the first, on the left, is filled with soya sauce, which the Chinese add to almost every sort of food; the second serves for ordinary eating; and in the third is a little spoon of porcelain for the soups. In front of these three cups, which are arranged in a line, lie two round ivory chop-sticks.

"As soon as the first course was removed, another small cup was added to each cover, to be used for drinking hot rice wine, offered by servants walking round with large silver cans.

"So soon as the first division of the dinner, consisting possibly of 60 ragouts, was over, the soups appeared; these were placed in small bowls in the middle of the table, and everyone ate, with his little porcelain spoon, out of the dish. In this way five or six different soups were served in succession, and between them various other things were placed before the guests in little cups; amongst these, pastry prepared in many ways, articles of confectionery, and strong chicken-hashes.

"Between the different grand divisions of the dinner, tea was handed round, and tobacco smoked.

"After several more courses, five small tables were placed outside of the half-circle of original tables; these were completely covered with roasted pork and birds of all sorts. Then ten cooks came into the room, clothed all alike and very tastefully, and began carving the roasts. Other servants, who stood in front of the tables, received the little bits upon small plates, and then placed them on the dining tables, to complete the repast."

CH. H. EDEN, *China, Historical & Descriptive*, 1880

A DICTIONARY
OF CHINESE CUISINE

Descriptions of exotic foodstuffs
(with their pronunciation in Cantonese)
and representative recipes

ABALONE, CANNED (Bow-Yew)   In China, most canned foods are looked down upon, but abalone is an exception, being more tasty than the fresh variety. The canned abalone found in the Chinatowns of the U.S. is a product of Mexico. It must be cooked as little as possible to prevent toughness.

ABALONE BRAISED IN OYSTER SAUCE (Ho-Yo Bow-Peen):

1 small can abalone
1 tsp. soya sauce
3 tbsp. Chinese oyster sauce

2 tsp. cornstarch
Chopped ham

Cut the abalone into thin slices 1-inch square. Mix the cornstarch with ⅓ cup of the abalone liquid, stirring until smooth. Sauté the abalone for 1 minute, then add the oyster, soya sauce, and cornstarch liquid. Sauté 2 minutes more, then transfer to warm serving dish. Sprinkle with the ham.

ABALONE AND BLACK MUSHROOM SOUP (Doan-Koo Bow-Yew Tong):

1 small can abalone
4 large dried black mushrooms
1 tbsp. soya sauce
1 cup pork tenderloin, diced

1 tsp. seasoning powder
1 tsp. salt
½ tsp. sesame oil

Soak the mushrooms in warm water for 15 minutes. Clean, squeeze dry, and cut into strips. Slice the abalone thin. Drain the juice of the canned abalone into a pot, add 5 cups water. Heat to boiling, then add the mushrooms and pork. Simmer 10 minutes, then add the abalone, soya sauce, seasoning powder, and salt. Simmer 2 minutes, then add the sesame oil. Do not overcook the abalone.

ABALONE, DRIED (Bow-Yew-Gawn)   The best dried abalone is produced in Japan. It is relished by the Chinese as a tasty and tender delicacy rich in nutrition.

PREPARATION OF DRIED ABALONE: ½ pound dried abalone will serve 10 people. Clean in warm water, then soak in cold water for 4 days, changing the water several times. When well softened and enlarged, put in an earthenware casserole with the following:

½ cup rice wine or sherry   1 cup hot water
 1 tbsp. peanut oil

Cover and cook in a slow oven for 5 hours, adding additional water when necessary. When quite tender, cut into slices and serve with the juice. Do not reheat the abalone once it has been sliced, or it will be tough.

AC'CENT   (*See* Seasoning Powder.)

AJINOMOTO (*See* Seasoning Powder.)

ALMONDS   Almonds are toasted and served as a sweetmeat, or used to garnish some dishes, particularly fowl.

ANCIENT EGGS   (*See* Eggs, Preserved.)

ANISEED   (*See* Five-Fragrance Spice Powder.)

APPETIZERS   (*See* Won Ton *and* Egg Rolls.)

ASPARAGUS

ASPARAGUS BRAISED WITH BEEF (Ching-Sun Ngow-Yuk):

½ lb. tenderloin of beef   1 lb. fresh young asparagus
 1 tbsp. soya sauce   1 garlic clove, minced
½ tsp. sugar   2 tbsp. soybean condiment

Slice the beef thin and mix with the soya sauce and sugar. Allow to stand 15 minutes. Wash asparagus and slice the tips obliquely; discard lower white portion. Sauté the garlic, then add the soybean condiment. Stir well, then add the asparagus. Cover and braise until asparagus turns light yellow. Place the beef mixture on top of the asparagus. Cover and cook 5 minutes longer. Season with salt, if necessary. Stir just when removing from fire.

BACON, UNCURED   (*See* Pork.)

BALSAM PEAR   (*See* Bitter Melon.)

BAMBOO SHOOTS (Jook Sun)   Cleaned and sliced bamboo shoots are available canned in the U.S. Canned whole bamboo shoots are imported from China, the best being the "winter shoots," and also from Japan (takenoko). Fresh bamboo shoots are available in some Chinatowns, being kept submerged in pails of water. These should be parboiled 15 minutes before using. Bamboo shoots are crunchy and possess a delicate flavor.

BAMBOO SHOOTS BRAISED WITH SLICED BREAST OF CHICKEN (Seen-Sun Gai-Peen):

1 pr. chicken breasts, skinned and boned
1½ cup bamboo shoots, fresh or canned
2 tbsp. soya sauce
½ tsp. sugar
¼ cup stock
2 tbsp. rice wine or sherry
1 tsp. salt

Cut the chicken breasts across the grain into thin slices. If fresh bamboo shoots are used, parboil them 15 minutes, drain well, then slice thin. Sauté the bamboo shoots for three minutes, then add the sliced chicken. Sauté for just one minute, then add the soya sauce, wine, sugar, salt, and stock. Continue sautéing for 2 minutes but do not overcook the chicken.

MARINATED FRESH BAMBOO SHOOTS (Im Bok-Sun):

½ lb. fresh bamboo shoots
1 tsp. sugar
2 tbsp. soya sauce
1 tbsp. sesame oil

Parboil the bamboo shoots 15 minutes. Drain, then slice thin. Place in a bowl, add the soya sauce, sugar, and sesame oil, and toss well. Allow to marinate for one hour, tossing occasionally.

BEAN CAKE   (*See* Bean Curd.)

71

BEAN CURD (Dou Foo)   Bean curd, one of the cheapest and most common of Chinese foods, can indeed be made into a delicacy. It has little flavor of its own, and can therefore be easily combined with other foods. It contains the same abundance of protein as the bean, but is more easily digested. It is made by cooking white soya beans to a purée, processing with calcium carbonate, filtering, then pressing into white cakes 4 inches square and 1 inch thick. This curd is highly perishable and should be parboiled before using.

BEAN CURD WITH MUSHROOMS IN OYSTER SAUCE (Ho-Yo Mo-Koo Dou-Foo):

4 cakes bean curd	¼ lb. fresh mushrooms
2 tbsp. Chinese oyster sauce	Chopped scallion

Cut each cake of bean curd into ½-inch pieces. Drop them into boiling water and simmer for 30 seconds, then drain them well. Slice the mushrooms thin, sauté them, then set aside. Heat about 3 teaspoons oil in a pan, then add the dry bean cake. Shake the pan, permitting the hot oil to coat all the pieces. Do not stir with any utensil, for that would break the curd. After a few minutes, pour in the oyster sauce. Continue shaking until the oyster sauce is thoroughly distributed. Add the sautéed mushrooms, shake well, and turn into a serving dish.

BEAN CURD BRAISED WITH PORK IN BROWN GRAVY (Hoong-Shew Dou-Foo):

4 cakes bean curd	1 tbsp. rice wine or sherry
2 tsp. soya sauce	1 large onion, sliced thin
1 tsp. sugar	½ cup stock
½ lb. tenderloin of pork	

Cut the bean curd into ½-inch pieces, then parboil them as in preceding recipe. Drain well. Cut the pork into small pieces. Brown in oil together with one mashed garlic clove. Season with the soya sauce, wine, and sugar. Add the bean curd and the onion. Stir in the stock, cover and cook for 5 minutes. Add a very small amount of cornstarch binder and stir lightly.

BEAN CURD CHEESE   Two varieties exist:

WHITE BEAN CURD CHEESE (Foo Yoo): Bean curd made from white soya beans is pressed and fermented in strong rice wine with salt. RED BEAN CURD CHEESE (Narm Yoo): Bean curd made from red soya beans is pressed and fermented in wine with salt. This is the more popular of the two in Cantonese cooking, frequently used in meat dishes, notably Pot Roast of Pork. It comes in small cans, and the cubes must be mashed together with the accompanying red sauce until smooth before using.

BEAN CURD, DRIED (Tim Jook)   Glazed stiff sheets of dried soya bean residue. Used in braised dishes, mostly fish, where it softens and becomes creamy smooth.

BEAN FILLING, SWEET (Doe Sha)   Black soya beans are boiled until tender, then mashed to a purée, combined with sugar and cooked slowly until thick and dry. Then a small amount of oil is beaten in. This sweet paste is available in Chinese bakeries, and is used in New Year's cakes and other sweet pastries.

BEAN SAUCE   (*See* Soya Bean Condiment.)

BEAN SPROUTS   (*See* Pea Sprouts.)

BEAR'S PAW   A delicacy unknown here, the bear's paw is a product of northern China. Its taste is unique, nearest to that of the best ham, without the greasiness, and when properly prepared melts in one's mouth. Highly nutritious.

BEEF   Tenderloin or sirloin are the cuts of beef mostly used in quick-cooking recipes, where the meat is cut in small pieces. Flank steak is excellent and economical. Beef plate, a muscular area near the brisket, is braised slowly to yield a tasty and tender dish. This cut of meat is termed "white abdomen of beef" (Ngow Bark Nahm).

BEEF PLATE BRAISED IN SOYA SAUCE (Hoong-Shew Ngow-Naam):

1 lb. beef plate	5 slices fresh ginger root
2 tbsp. rice wine or sherry	¼ cup soya sauce
1 tbsp. sugar	Stock or hot water

73

Cut the beef plate into 1-inch cubes. Parboil them a few minutes, then drain well. Place in a casserole together with the ginger, wine, soya sauce, and sugar. Add enough stock or water to barely cover the meat. Cover and simmer very slowly for about three hours, or until the muscular tendons are very soft.

BELL PEPPERS   (*See* Peppers, Bell.)

BINDER   (*See* Cornstarch.)

BIRD'S NEST   (*See* Swallow's Nest.)

BITTER MELON (Foo-Gwa)   Also called the balsam pear (Momordica charantta), a vegetable the size of a cucumber, with a green wrinkled skin. Its flavor is cool and slightly bitter, owing to the presence of quinine, to which one must accustom oneself. It is used in soup, braised with meat, and stuffed. Available fresh in Chinatown; also canned.

BITTER MELON BRAISED WITH BEEF (Foo-Gwa Ngow-Yuk):

1 lb. fresh bitter melon	1 garlic clove
¼ lb. beef tenderloin, sliced thin	2 tsp. soya sauce
2 tsp. fermented black soya beans	2 tbsp. rice wine or sherry
½ tsp. sugar	¾ cup stock

Cut the bitter melon in half, remove seeds, then cut the melon into thin slices. Parboil for 3 minutes, then drain well. Wash the black beans, drain, then mash together with the garlic. Heat oil in a pan, add the garlic-bean pulp and stir for ½ minute. Add the bitter melon and sauté 2 minutes. Add the beef and sauté 1 minute. Add the soya sauce, sugar, and wine. Season with salt, then add the stock. Braise for 1 minute. Thicken with cornstarch binder.

BLACK BEAN SAUCE   (*See* Soya Beans, Black Fermented.)

BLACK BEANS   (*See* Soya Beans, Black Fermented)

BLACK VINEGAR   (*See* Vinegar.)

BRAISING   (*See* Cooking, Chinese Methods of.)

BRINJAL, HAIRY   (*See* Hairy Melon.)

BROCOLLI   Brocolli must be young and sliced obliquely for Chinese cooking. The Chinese variety is much more leafy.

BROWN BEAN SAUCE   (*See* Soya Bean Condiment.)

CABBAGE, CELERY (Wong-Nga-Bok)   This is the tall, yellow-white, closely leaved vegetable often found in American markets. It is used raw in Occidental cookery as salad, but as a cooked vegetable it is delicious.

CELERY CABBAGE SAUTÉ: Use recipe for Chinese cabbage sauté.

CABBAGE, CHINESE (Bok-Choy)   The name Chinese cabbage is often incorrectly applied to the celery cabbage, which is quite another vegetable. Chinese cabbage, termed "white cabbage" in the native language, is a slender vegetable of succulent white stems with dark green leaves at the tops, resembling Swiss chard somewhat. It is found in Chinatown only. The inner hearts sometimes are sold separately.

CHINESE CABBAGE SAUTÉ (Chow Bok-Choy):

1 small head Chinese cabbage	1 tsp. salt
½ tsp. sugar	1 tsp. soya sauce
2 tbsp. rice wine or sherry	⅓ cup hot water

Wash the cabbage, then slice the stems obliquely into 1-inch lengths. Keep the leaves separate. Sauté the white stems 2 minutes, then add the green leaves. Sauté another minute. Sprinkle with the salt and sugar, then add the soya sauce, wine, and hot water. Stir, cover, and cook 2 minutes longer. Do not overcook, or the cabbage will lose its crunchiness.

CHINESE CABBAGE SOUP (Bok-Choy Tong):

1 small head Chinese cabbage, sliced thin	1 tsp. salt
	½ tsp. sugar
¼ lb. raw lean pork, chopped	4 cups hot water
3 slices fresh ginger root	2 tsp. soya sauce

Sauté the ginger a minute, then add the hot water and salt. Bring to boil, stir in the cabbage. Simmer covered for 10 minutes. Add the pork, sugar, and soya sauce. Season with pepper. Cover and simmer 15 minutes longer.

CABBAGE, DRIED CHINESE (Bock Choy Gawn) Dried Chinese cabbage is used in soups and stews, imparting a unique flavor.

CABBAGE, PRESERVED The Chinese mustard cabbage, Brassica cernua, is preserved with salt in various ways, each with its individual taste, according to the condiments used.

SALTED MUSTARD GREENS (Harm Choy) in cans and bulk
    var. Onion pickled (Choan Choy) in bulk
        Fermented (Mooey Choy) in jars
        "Winter vegetable" (Doan Choy) in cans
        "Red-inside-snow" (Sewt Lay Hoan)

When purchased from bulk, the cabbage must be washed clean, squeezed dry, and sliced. Preserved cabbage is steamed or sautéed with meat and fish, and used in soups.

MINCED PORK STEAMED WITH SALTED CABBAGE (Doan-Choy Jing-Yuk):

½ lb. pork tenderloin, chopped coarsely	1 tsp. cornstarch
	1 tsp. peanut oil
¼ cup "winter vegetable" salted cabbage	1 tsp. soya sauce

Chop the cabbage fine, then combine with all ingredients. Mix well, then form into a thin pancake in a dish. Place the dish in a steamer and steam for 30 minutes.

CALTROPS   (*See* Water Chestnut.)

CANDIED GINGER   (*See* Ginger.)

CAUL FAT (Mong Yo)   Caul fat is the thin net-like membrane covering the lower portion of pigs' intestines. Used for wrapping foods to be steamed or fried.

CELERY   Celery is sliced obliquely very thin, and used in chow yuks and sautéed dishes.

CELERY CABBAGE   (*See* Cabbage, Celery.)

CELLOPHANE NOODLES   (*See* Noodles.)

CHEESE, RED   (*See* Bean Curd Cheese.)

CHESTNUTS (Loot Jee)   Shelled, dried chestnut halves are available in Chinatown.

CHICKEN BRAISED WITH CHESTNUTS (Lewt-Jee Gai):

½ spring chicken	½ lb. dried chestnuts
2 tbsp. soya sauce	½ tsp. sugar
1 tsp. fresh ginger root, minced	2 tbsp. rice wine or sherry
1 tsp. salt	2 cups boiling water

Parboil the chestnuts 10 minutes, then peel off the skins. Chop the chicken into small pieces, bones included. Brown the chicken, then season with the soya sauce, sugar, ginger, wine, and salt. Add the chestnuts, then pour in the boiling water. Stir, cover, and simmer for one hour, or until both chicken and chestnuts are tender.

CHESTNUTS, WATER   (*See* Water Chestnuts.)

CHICKEN   Chicken with Litchis & Pineapple (*See* Litchi.)
Chicken with Chestnuts (*See* Chestnuts.)
Chicken with Walnuts (*See* Walnuts.)
Chicken with Peppers (*See* Peppers, Chili.)

PAPER-WRAPPED CHICKEN (Jee-Bow Gai):

1 pair chicken breasts	1 tbsp. soya sauce
2 tsp. sweet vegetable sauce	1 tsp. sugar
1 tbsp. rice wine or sherry	½ tsp. sesame oil
½ cup scallions, chopped	Tissue or wax paper

Skin the chicken breasts, then cut them across the grain into thick slices. Combine the remaining ingredients, add the chicken and toss. Season with salt. Allow to stand 15 minutes. Cut tissue paper into 4-inch squares. On each square lay one piece of chicken then wrap up securely so that packet is well closed. Fry the packets in deep fat until golden brown.

CHILI PEPPERS   (*See* Peppers, Chili.)

CHINESE CABBAGE   (*See* Cabbage, Chinese.)

CHINKIANG VINEGAR   (*See* Vinegar.)

CHOP SUEY   Literally, "miscellaneous bits." A made-up dish originally prepared by Chinese immigrants in the U.S. for Americans. It has many variations, but usually consists of strips of pork sautéed with bean sprouts, celery, bamboo shoots, water chestnut, mushrooms, and onion.

CHOW MEIN   Literally, "fried noodles." Chow mein is a dish of browned noodles served with mixed sautéed vegetables; a sort of chop suey with noodles. The crisp sort of noodle served in American-Chinese restaurants is unknown in China.

CHOW YUK   Literally, "fried pork." This term designates any sautéed dish of finely-cut pork with one or more vegetables.

CINNAMON   (*See* Five-Fragrance Spice Powder.)

"CLOUD EARS" FUNGUS   (*See* Fungus, Dried.)

CLOVE   (*See* Five-Fragrance Spice Powder.)

COCONUT   Coconut meat is cut into strips and boiled in sugar syrup, then crystallized for use as sweetmeat.

CONGEE   Rice gruel made by boiling rice until a smooth broth is formed. Sometimes other ingredients are added, such as duck or pork. It is served most often together with pickles and sliced fish, as a breakfast dish.

COOKING, CHINESE METHODS OF

THE SAUTÉ: The Chinese sauté is similar to that of French cookery, however in no case is the food allowed to brown. A very high heat is used, and the thinly-sliced meat and vegetables are lightly tossed in a minimum amount of peanut oil, the meat being generally added first and then the vegetables. Cooking is continued until the vegetables just begin to lose their "crunchiness." They must not be allowed to cook to the tender stage, as in Occidental cookery. This method of cooking preserves the color, texture, and taste of the ingredients. It is a rapid form of cooking, and there is generally little juice. Sometimes the ingredients are separately prepared by partially cooking, such as parboiling and light sautéing, then combined for final cooking.

BRAISING OR STEWING: In this method, the ingredients are first sautéed, or sometimes deep-fried. Seasonings and a small amount of stock or water are then added, the pan is covered, and the food is allowed to simmer slowly. The sauce is sometimes thickened with cornstarch binder before serving. If soya sauce is heavily used, giving the dish a rich red-brown color, the process is called "red stewing."

STEAMING: The steaming process preserves the natural quality of the raw ingredients better than any other method of cooking. Fresh fish is best cooked by steaming.

A large pot having a tight-fitting lid is required. Two to 3 inches of boiling water is poured into the pot, and a rack is suspended over the water. The dish or bowl containing the food is placed on the rack. The water is kept at a minimum boil, and the cooking time can range from 20 minutes to 5 hours, depending on the dish steamed.

ROASTING: Roasting in Chinese cookery is done in ovens over a charcoal fire. Basting is done frequently.

DEEP-FRYING: Ingredients are deep-fried usually as a preliminary step to stewing, but some foods, such as chicken and fish, are first marinated in sauce, then coated with cornstarch or flour and deep-fried until tender and a light golden brown.

CORNSTARCH   Cornstarch is used as a thickening agent in Chinese cooking in America. In China, waterchestnut flour and pea flour are used. Before being added to a recipe, it must be mixed with a little water to a smooth paste, otherwise it would cause the dish to be lumpy. The sauces of most epicurean Chinese dishes are not thickened to excess, as is often the case in the Cantonese-American school, where the majority of dishes is bogged down in a thick gravy. Cornstarch is also used to rub on the surface of meats before cooking. This seals in the juices and produces a rich golden-brown surface color. The term *cornstarch* refers to the dry starch; *cornstarch binder* designates a smooth paste of cornstarch and water.

CRAB   CURRIED CANTONESE CRAB (Ka-Lei Hi-Yuk): Remove shell of crab and chop crab into small pieces. Crack claws. Use recipe for Cantonese Lobster (see Lobster), adding curry powder to taste.

CUCUMBER   Cucumber may be substituted for bitter melon, hairy melon, and loofah gourd.

CUCUMBER PICKLE   (*See* Tea Melon.)

CUTTLEFISH   (*See* Squid.)

DEEP-FRYING   (*See* Cooking, Chinese Methods of.)

DISHCLOTH GOURD   (*See* Loofah Gourd.)

DOILIES   Thin wheat cakes baked from unraised dough. Used in northern China as bread. Food is placed on the doilie, which is rolled up and eaten with the fingers. Most popularly served with Peking Roast Duck. Wheat tortillas make a perfect substitute.

DRAGON'S EYES   (*See* Lungan.)

DRIED DUCK   (*See* Duck, Preserved.)

DUCK, PRESERVED   Also called pressed duck, two types exist: SALT DRIED DUCK (Larp Op): Salted and pressed flat, then dried in the sun. OIL PRESERVED SALTED DUCK (Yo Jum Larp Op): Salted and pressed flat, then immersed in peanut oil. To use either variety, first wash with cold water, chop into small pieces and steam until tender, about 30 minutes.

DUCK, ROAST   CANTONESE ROAST DUCK (Shew-Aap):

1 tender whole duck, head attached	½ cup honey
1 garlic clove, minced	2 tsp. sugar
1 tsp. salt	2 tbsp. rice wine or sherry
1 tsp. minced fresh ginger root	1 cup stock or water
2 scallions, chopped	Soya sauce

Clean the duck, slitting it at the back and removing intestines. Dry the duck thoroughly with paper towels. Combine the garlic, sugar, salt, wine, ginger, scallions, and 2 tablespoons soya sauce. Add the stock or water. Bring the mixture to a boil, then pour boiling into the duck, sewing up the opening so that none of the mixture leaks out. Hang the duck up by the neck. Combine the honey with ¼ cup soya sauce, then pour this mixture over the duck six times or more. Place the duck on a rack in a pan containing a shallow amount of water. Roast at 400° until the duck is browned, about 20 minutes, then turn duck and lower heat to 275°. Roast 30 minutes longer, basting with the drippings. Turn heat off and allow duck to remain in oven for 20 minutes. Cut the duck open and allow sauce to drain into bowl. Disjoint the duck, arrange on serving dish and pour the sauce over. Also delicious served cold.

Cantonese Roast Duck can also be purchased ready-cooked in Chinatown.

PEKING ROAST DUCK (Ging-Gerng Aap):

1 tender whole duck, head attached	1 cup boiling water
½ cup honey	1 tsp. five-fragrance spice
1 tsp. salt	2 tbsp. rice wine or sherry
3 tbsp. red vegetable sauce	1 tsp. distilled vinegar
1 tsp. sugar	Chinese plum sauce

Clean the duck, then submerge it in boiling water for 1 minute. Drain and dry the skin with paper towels. Combine the honey and boiling water and rub into the skin of the duck until thoroughly imbued. Rub the inside of the duck with the salt and the spice powder. Hang up the duck by the neck and allow to dry for 10 hours, until the skin is hard. Combine the red vegetable sauce, wine, sugar, and vinegar and rub inside the duck. Roast the duck, preferably over an open barbecue, or as for Cantonese Roast Duck. Serve with Chinese Plum Sauce.

DUCK SAUCE   (*See* Plum Sauce.)

DUCKS' FEET   Considered by some people the most delicious part of the duck. Ducks' feet are readily available in Chinatown. They are an important ingredient in soup stock.

DUCKS' FEET BRAISED WITH MUSHROOMS, BAMBOO SHOOTS AND WATER CHESTNUTS (Hoong-Shew Aap-Gerk):

10 pair ducks' feet	½ cup sliced bamboo shoots
4 large dried black mushrooms, soaked and cleaned	1 cup stock
½ cup sliced water chestnuts	½ tsp. sugar
1 tbsp. soya sauce	2 tbsp. rice wine or sherry
	Cornstarch binder

Clean the ducks' feet, then soak them in boiling water for 5 minutes. Remove and discard the skin, clip off the claws, then pull all the bones, cutting each foot into two pieces. Sauté the feet for 5 minutes, then add the bamboo shoots, mushrooms, and water chestnut. Sauté 5 minutes more. Add the soya sauce, sugar, and wine. Season with salt, then add the stock. Simmer until the feet are tender. Thicken the broth with cornstarch binder.

EGG ROLLS   Use whole won ton skins. Fill each with 2 tablespoons egg roll filling and roll up into a tight roll, moistening edge to seal. Fry them in deep fat until golden. Serve hot.

EGG ROLL FILLING:

½ cup cooked pork, chopped
½ cup cooked shrimp, chopped
½ cup celery, chopped

½ cup water chestnuts, chopped
½ cup bamboo shoots, chopped
1 cup bean sprouts

Sauté the vegetables and season with soya sauce, sugar, salt, and pepper. Drain and cool before using.

EGGS, PRESERVED   There are two types of preserved egg, the lime-treated and the salt-treated. Both are cured for less than 100 days. Ducks' eggs are usually employed.

LIME-TREATED EGGS (Pay Don): The eggs are coated with a paste of ashes, lime, and salt. They are packed in earth and allowed to cure for about 100 days. Available in Chinatown.

Preparation: Remove the ash covering, wash and shell the eggs. Slice each egg into 4 quarters. Arrange on a dish and serve with oyster sauce, soya sauce, or pickled ginger.

SALT-TREATED EGGS (Harm Don): These are preserved in a pure salt coating, but the inside of the egg is not congealed, as with the lime-treated egg. Available in Chinatown.

Preparation: Remove salt covering and wash eggs. Boil slowly for 30 minutes; shell, slice, and serve with hot peanut oil.

Note that the lime-treated eggs are not to be cooked, while the salt-treated are.

EGGPLANT   EGGPLANT BRAISED WITH BEEF (Kair-Jee Ngow-Yuk):

1 firm medium eggplant	2 tsp. soya sauce
½ lb. tenderloin of beef	½ tsp. sugar
1 tsp. fresh ginger root, minced	2 tbsp. red bean sauce

Cut the beef into thin slices and mix with the soya sauce, red bean sauce, and sugar. Allow to marinate for 15 minutes. Peel eggplant and slice thin. Sauté the minced ginger, then add the eggplant. Sauté 2 minutes. Place the beef mixture on top of the eggplant; do not stir. Cover and braise slowly 5 to 10 minutes. Season with salt and stir during last minute of cooking.

FENNEL   (*See* Five-Fragrance Spice Powder.)

FERMENTED BLACK BEANS   (*See* Soya Beans, Black Fermented.)

FISH MAW (Yew Toe)   The stomach lining of certain fish is dried, deep-fried, then hung above one's head in the grocery shops of Chinatown. It is similar in texture to pork rind. Used in soups and stews.

FISH MAW IN CHICKEN BROTH (Ching-Tong Yew-To.)

¼ lb. fish maw	½ tsp. distilled vinegar
6 cups chicken stock	1 tbsp. rice wine
1 tsp. ginger juice	1 egg, beaten
Cornstarch binder	Chopped ham
½ cup water chestnuts	

Soak the fish maw in cold water for 3 hours. It will increase in volume four times. Drain, then add to boiling water together with the distilled vinegar, ginger juice, and wine. Simmer 5 minutes. Drain and wash in cold water, removing all traces of oil. Squeeze dry. Cut into small pieces. Heat the chicken stock, add the fish maw and water chestnuts. Simmer 30 minutes. Thicken the soup slightly with cornstarch binder. Remove from fire and gradually stir in the beaten egg. Serve at once, garnishing with ham.

FISH, SALTED (Hom Yew)   Several varieties of fish are salted and dried. They are usually steamed with rice or with pork. (*See* recipe, Minced Pork Steamed with Water Chestnuts, under "Water Chestnuts." Lay several washed slices of salted fish on top of the meat cake before steaming.)

FIVE-FLOWER PORK   (*See* Pork.)

FIVE-FRAGRANCE SPICE POWDER   A blend of five aromatic spices.
   STAR ANISE (Baat Gawk): So called because its brown seed is in the shape of an eight-pointed star.
   FENNEL (Aniseed).
   SZECHUAN PEPPER (Fa Jew): Only faintly hot.
   CLOVE.
   CHINESE CINNAMON.

These five spices are ground together to a fine powder and sold under the name Herng Lew Fun. They are also available whole. If this spice powder is unobtainable, an adequate substitute can be made as follows:

1 tsp. powdered cinnamon   1 tsp. powdered aniseed
1 tsp. powdered cloves   1 tsp. powdered thyme

This spice should be used subtly.

FORTUNE COOKIES   Rice wafers are prepared from a batter consisting of flour, powdered sugar, eggs, and banana flavoring. The batter is poured on hot grills and toasted to make thin round wafers. Strips of fortune paper are placed on the wafers while still hot and the cookies are folded up from 3 sides.

FRAGRANT SPICES   (*See* Five-Fragrance Spice Powder.)

FROGS' LEGS   FROGS' LEGS BRAISED WITH WINTER MELON (Doan-Gwa Tin-Gai):

8 pair dressed frogs' legs	½ cup stock
½ lb. piece winter melon	2 tbsp. rice wine or sherry
2 large dried Chinese mushrooms	Cornstarch
1 garlic clove, minced	Sesame oil

Pare the melon and cut the meat into ½-inch cubes. Soak the dried mushrooms; cut into strips. Sprinkle the frogs' legs with salt, then dust with cornstarch. Fry in deep fat until light golden; drain. Keep warm. Sauté the garlic, add the winter melon and mushrooms. Sauté 2 minutes, then add the wine and stock. Cover and braise 5 minutes. Add the frogs' legs and heat through. Transfer to serving dish and sprinkle with a few drops of sesame oil.

FRUITS, PRESERVED   Fruits are preserved with sugar or honey, some flavored with licorice, some with clove, others with ginger. They are eaten as a confection, or used in desserts. Commonly found: sugar-preserved winter melon, clove-flavored plums, glacé orange rind, preserved kumquat, dried litchi, preserved wongpay (yellow skin), spiced ginger.

STEAMED RICE PUDDING WITH PRESERVED FRUITS (Bot-Bo Fahn):

3 cups cooked rice (1 cup uncooked)	Assorted sweet preserved fruits
¼ cup sugar	Almonds
¼ cup butter (½ cube)	

Combine the cooked rice and sugar. Grease an aluminum pan generously. Arrange a layer of fruits and almonds in the bottom of the pan, then cover with a layer of rice. Repeat layers until pan is full, ending with a layer of rice. Place the pan in a steamer and steam 40 minutes. Turn out onto a plate and serve hot.

FU YUNG   Literally "hibiscus," this term designates several dishes of meat, seafood, or vegetables, all prepared with beaten egg. The food is cooked into a solid thick pancake, and most Fu Yung dishes contain bean sprouts. In Chinese *haute cuisine*, only the white of the egg is used.

FUNGUS, DRIED: The dried cultivated edible fungus, auricularia auricula judae, possesses high tonic qualities.

WHITE FUNGUS (Sewt Yee), also called Snow Fungus.
BROWN FUNGUS (Wun Yee), also called Cloud Ears.
They are used in soups, in braised dishes and vegetarian dishes.

SNOW FUNGUS IN CHICKEN BROTH (Ching-Tong Sewt-Yee):

2 oz. dried white fungus	5 cups chicken stock
¼ cup bamboo shoots, sliced then diced	1 tsp. seasoning powder
2 large dried mushrooms	

Soak the fungus in warm water for 30 minutes, then clean, rinse, and squeeze dry. Soak the mushrooms 15 minutes, then cut into strips. Heat the soup stock and add the fungus, bamboo shoots, and mushrooms. Boil slowly for 25 minutes, then add the seasoning powder. Season with salt.

GINGER   Fresh ginger root (Gerng), a hot spicy tuber, is available in Chinatown and in some American markets. It is indispensable in Chinese cuisine, and the dried ground variety must not be used as a substitute; better to omit it from recipe altogether. Ginger is used particularly in fish cookery to alleviate any strong taste or odor. Ginger is pickled together with carrots, turnips, onions and cucumbers. This is available in jars (Sup Kum Gerng), and used in sweet-sour dishes. Ginger is also available sliced and candied, either crystallized or in syrup.

GINGKO NUT (Bok Gwaw)   These are available canned or dried. If dried ones are used, crack the shells with a nutcracker, then soak the nuts in hot water for 10 minutes. Peel off the inner skin. The gingko nut is used in soups, notably the whole winter melon soup. It is also an important ingredient in vegetarian dishes, and where a recipe calls for a numerous list of mixed ingredients, such as festival dishes.

GINSENG (Yun Sharm)   The ginseng root, panax gingseng, is considered in China the most efficacious of tonics. It is costly and can be purchased from any Chinese herb shop and some grocery stores. Be sure to specify it is for soup.

SQUAB SOUP WITH GINSENG (Yun-Sharm Bok-Gop Tong):

2 squabs, cleaned
⅓ cup rice wine or sherry
1 slice fresh ginger root

1 tsp. soya sauce
½ cup ginseng root
5 cups soup stock

Slice the ginseng root. Disjoint the squabs. Heat the soup stock, add the squab and wine. Simmer 20 minutes. Add the ginseng, ginger, and soya sauce. Continue to simmer for 45 minutes. Season with salt and seasoning powder.

GOLDEN NEEDLES   (*See* Lilies, Dried Tiger.)

GRASS MUSHROOMS   (*See* Mushrooms, Dried Chinese.)

GRAVY, CHINESE BROWN   This term refers to the ingredients usually added to a dish near the end of the cooking period. The following is a basic recipe, but of course is variable, according to the seasoning desired:

2 cups stock (or water)
1 tsp. soya sauce
2 tsp. cornstarch (made into a paste)

(Plus salt, sugar, seasoning powder, pepper, etc.)

If prepared separately, cook until thickened. If added to a dish being cooked, allow to thicken with the other ingredients.

GREEN ONIONS   (*See* Onions.)

HAIR SEAWEED   (*See* Seaweed.)

HAIRY MELON (Jick Gwa *or* Moe Gwa)   A longitudinal green vegetable marrow with fine white fuzz on the skin. Also called hairy brinjal, it is available fresh in season in Chinatown. It is similar to cucumber, which makes a fine substitute.

SOUP WITH HAIRY MELON AND CHICKEN (Mo-Gwa Gai-Peen Tong):

1 large hairy melon	1 tsp. soya sauce
1 cup diced chicken meat	1 tsp. seasoning powder
5 cups soup stock	

Pare the hairy melon, then cut the melon into ½-inch dice. Add the melon and chicken to the boiling soup stock. Simmer 15 minutes, then season with the soya sauce, seasoning powder, and salt if necessary.

HAM   Fine aged Smithfield ham bears the closest resemblance to Chinese ham.

HERBS   The following herbs, all nutrient tonics, are used in Chinese cooking. They are available at any herb shop and at most Chinese grocery shops.

GINSENG (*See* under Ginseng).
RED BERRIES (Go Jee): Lycium chinense.
SWEET ROOT (Why Shon).

CHICKEN SOUP WITH CHINESE HERBS (Go-Jee Why-Shon Gai-Tong):

2 cups chicken meat, cubed	5 cups soup stock
¼ cup red berries	¼ cup rice wine or sherry
¼ cup sweet root	Seasoning powder

Soak the herbs in cold water for 30 minutes, wash and drain. Heat the soup stock, add the chicken and simmer 10 minutes. Add the herbs and rice wine, cover and simmer for 45 minutes. Season with salt, pepper, and seasoning powder.

HUNDRED-YEAR-OLD EGGS   (*See* Eggs, Preserved.)

JUJUBE, DRIED: There are three types: RED DATES (Hoan Jo), WHITE HONEY DATES (Mut Jo), and BLACK DATES (Huk Jo). They all have a sweet flavor when cooked in soups, fish dishes and desserts. Red dates are the most common. All must be soaked for one hour before using.

KUMQUAT   A small yellow fruit of the citrus family, Citrus nobilis, slightly acid with a strong orange flavor and odor. Usually preserved in sugar syrup and served as a sweetmeat (Mut Gum Gwut).

LAVER   (*See* Seaweed.)

LILIES, DRIED TIGER (Gum Jum)   The dried flower of the tiger lily is most often used in conjunction with fungus or other dried ingredients, notably in vegetarian dishes. These nutritious dried buds are gold in color and are called "golden needles" in Chinese.

CHICKEN BRAISED WITH TIGER LILIES (Gum-Jum Gai):

1 frying chicken, disjointed	2 tbsp. rice wine or sherry
1 doz. dried tiger lilies	1 tsp. fresh ginger root, minced
4 dried Chinese mushrooms	1 cup stock
1 tbsp. soya sauce	

Soak the dried lilies and mushrooms separately in warm water for 15 minutes. Clean, rinse, and squeeze dry. Slice the mushrooms into strips. Brown the chicken, then add the soya sauce, wine, and ginger. Add the lilies, mushrooms, and stock. Stir, cover, and braise until the chicken is tender.

LITCHI (Lay Jee)   Also, Lychee. Indigenous to south China, the litchi tree, Nephelium litchi, bears a fruit which looks like a large red strawberry. The thin shell-like red skin encloses a milky white, translucent pulp which is very sweet, delicate in flavor and refreshing. Skinned and seeded litchis are available canned (See Lay Jee) for use as dessert fruit or in sweet chicken or duck dishes. When dehydrated, the skins turn a rich brownish red and become hard, while the white meat inside shrivels around the seed, turns dark, and tastes somewhat like raisins. These are the litchi "nuts" (Lay Jee Gon) popular in the U.S. as sweetmeat. The yellow blossoms of the litchi are used to perfume tea.

SLICED BREAST OF CHICKEN WITH LITCHI & PINEAPPLE (Lay-Jee Bo-Lo Gai):

2 pair chicken breasts	½ cup canned pineapple chunks
1 tbsp. soya sauce	½ cup canned litchis
2 tbsp. rice wine or sherry	½ cup pineapple juice
1 tsp. minced fresh ginger root	½ cup litchi juice

Skin the chicken breasts, then slice across the grain as thin as possible. Sauté the chicken until the slices curl up, then add the soya sauce, wine, and ginger. Add the pineapple and litchi and braise 2 minutes. Add the pineapple and litchi juice. When the sauce comes to a boil, thicken with cornstarch binder. Serve at once.

LOBSTER

LOBSTER CANTONESE (She-Jup Loong-Har):

1 live lobster	1 cup stock
1 cup lean pork, chopped	1 egg, beaten
2 tbsp. fermented black beans, crushed	Rice wine or sherry
1 garlic clove, minced	Cornstarch binder

Cut the cleaned lobster through the shell into 1-inch pieces; cut claws in half. Sauté the pork, black beans, and garlic about 2 minutes. Add the lobster and season with salt, pepper, sugar, and rice wine. Add the stock, stir, then cover and simmer for 5 minutes, or until lobster is done. Thicken sauce with cornstarch binder, then remove from heat and stir in the beaten egg. Serve at once.

LONG RICE   (*See* Noodles.)

LOOFAH GOURD (Sze Gwa)   Also known as snake squash and dishcloth gourd, the loofah gourd, Luffa cylindrica, is a slender fruit of the curcurbitacae family. Cucumber will do as a substitute.

LOQUAT (Pay Pa Gwor)   The small yellow fruit of Eriobotrya japonica, which grows in clusters on the tree. The surface of the fruit possesses a fine fuzz. Sour and juicy. Preserved and served as a sweetmeat.

LOTUS CAKES (Leen Yoan Beng)   Small baked pie-crust cakes filled with lotus jam. Available in Chinese bakeries.

LOTUS JAM (Leen Yoan)   A thick mixture of lotus seeds boiled with sugar. Used as a filling in Lotus Cakes and other pastries.

LOTUS LEAVES   When fresh, lotus leaves impart their flavor and fragrance to food. The dried leaves are used in China for wrapping food.

LOTUS ROOT (Leen Ngow)   The starchy root of the aquatic lily Nelumbo nucifera is reddish-brown in color. It is about 2 inches in diameter and has a joint every foot or so of its length. Sliced crosswise, it reveals an interior of holes running vertically throughout each length. They are available fresh in Chinatown.

LOTUS ROOT SOUP (Leen-Ngow Tong):

1 lb. fresh lotus root	1 tsp. salt
½ lb. stewing beef or beef plate	5 cups boiling water
3 slices fresh ginger root	1 tsp. seasoning powder

Cut the beef into ½-inch cubes. Pare the lotus root, then cut in ¼-inch slices. Heat the water to boiling and add the lotus root, beef, and ginger. Cover and simmer 3 hours. Add the salt and simmer ½ hour longer. Correct salt seasoning, then add pepper and seasoning powder to taste.

SLICED LOTUS ROOT BRAISED WITH PORK (Leen-Ngow Chow-Yuk):

1 lb. fresh lotus root	1 tbsp. soya sauce
½ lb. pork tenderloin	½ cup stock
2 tbsp. rice wine or sherry	

Wash and pare the lotus root. Cut into thin slices. Cut the pork into thin strips. Sauté the pork until lightly browned. Add the sliced lotus root and sauté 2 minutes. Add the wine and soya sauce. Season with salt. Add the stock, cover and braise 5 minutes.

LOTUS SEEDS (Leen Jee)   Lotus seeds come canned or as dried nuts with dark-brown husks. They are used in sweet dishes, as dessert, and in making lotus jam filling for pastries.

LOTUS SEEDS IN CHICKEN BROTH (Ching-Tong Leen-Jee):

½ lb. dried lotus seeds	¼ cup green peas
4 cups rich chicken stock	1 tsp. sugar
½ cup sliced chicken meat	1 tbsp. chopped ham
½ cup button mushrooms, sliced	

Blanch the lotus seeds in boiling water, then allow to soak in the lukewarm water for 15 minutes. Rub off the brown husks, wash and drain. Return the seeds to boiling water and boil slowly for 20 minutes. Drain. Heat the chicken stock and add the chicken meat, mushrooms, sugar, and the lotus seeds. Cover and simmer very gently for 30 minutes. Add the green peas and cook 5 minutes longer. Pour into serving bowl and sprinkle with the chopped ham.

LUNGAN   A fruit of southern China, Nephelium longana, the lungan, also called "Dragon's Eyes," is available dried or canned. It is used as a sweet dessert fruit.

CANNED LUNGAN (Seen Loan-Ngon).
DRIED LUNGAN (Loan Ngon-Gon).

LYCHEE   (*See* Litchi.)

MARROW, VEGETABLE   (*See* Hairy Melon.)

MAW, FISH   (*See* Fish Maw.)

MEE BOAN   (*See* Seasoning Powder.)

MELON   (*See* Hairy Melon; Winter Melon; Bitter Melon.)

93

MELON SEEDS (Hoan Gwa Jee) "The" sweetmeat of the Chinese. Experience is required to dexterously crack open the shells and extract the kernel, all done with the teeth. Dried from the common watermelon.

MOON CAKES Small baked cakes filled with various stuffings, some with meat, chicken, and vegetables, others with sweet bean filling, lotus jam, nuts, sesame seeds, and preserved melon. They are available at Chinese bakeries during the Moon Festival (15th of 8th Moon).

MUSHROOMS, DRIED CHINESE There are several varieties of dried Chinese mushrooms, two of which are:

WINTER MUSHROOM (Doan Koo): Black-Capped, up to 2 inches in diameter. Most commonly used.
GRASS MUSHROOM (Cho Koo): Tall and thin, very tasty.

Dried mushrooms are a very savory addition to many recipes. They are available in Chinatown, and are moderately expensive. Before using, they must be soaked in warm water for 15 minutes, rinsed, then squeezed dry.

MUSTARD The best mustard for use in Chinese cookery is the powdered English variety, freshly mixed to a smooth paste.

MUSTARD GREENS, CHINESE (Guy Choy) The Chinese mustard cabbage, Brassica cernue, is green with yellow flowers on the tops of the central stem. It is slightly bitter in taste. Available in Chinatown. It is sautéed or served in soup.

MUSTARD GREENS SOUP (Gai-Choi Tong):

1 head mustard cabbage	5 cups soup stock
½ cup pork, cut small	1 tsp. soya sauce
4 slices fresh ginger root	1 tsp. seasoning powder

Wash and slice the mustard cabbage obliquely. Heat the soup stock, add ginger and pork. Boil 5 minutes. Add mustard cabbage and boil 3 minutes. Season with the soya sauce, seasoning powder, and with salt and pepper.

NET FAT   (*See* Caul Fat.)

NEW YEAR'S CAKES (Jeen Duy)   Globular cakes of rice flour and brown sugar, filled with sweet bean filling. They are rolled in sesame seeds and deep fried. Available at Chinese bakeries, mostly during the Chinese New Year.

NOODLES   Wheat noodles are the staple food of northern China. They are served in broth, or sautéed with other ingredients to form Chow Mein. The crisp noodles served in American-Chinese restaurants are not found in China.

EGG NOODLES, FRESH (Don Meen).

EGG NOODLES, DRIED (Gawn Don-Meen).

OCHRE-COLORED VERMICELLI (Yee-Foo Meen).

"POWDERED SILK" VERMICELLI (Fun See): Also called "long rice" noodles, and "cellophane" noodles. Made from mungo beans. Translucent.

Boil fresh egg noodles for 10 minutes; dried noodles for 20 minutes. Rinse in cold water, then add to broth or other dishes.

SOUP WITH "POWERED SILK" VERMICELLI & CHICKEN (Fun-See Gai-See Tong):

½ bunch "powdered silk" vermicelli   1 tsp. soya sauce
 1 cup chopped chicken meat   Chopped scallion
 5 cups soup stock

Soak the vermicelli in cold water for 30 minutes. Cut into 3-inch lengths. Heat the soup stock, add the vermicelli and chicken meat. Cover and boil slowly for 20 minutes, then add the soya sauce. Correct salt seasoning and add seasoning powder if desired. Garnish with chopped scallion.

OIL, COOKING   In China, bean oil, rape seed oil, sesame seed oil, and peanut oil are used as cooking fat. Peanut oil is available in the U.S. and is preferred to butter or other solid vegetable fats for Chinese cooking.

OLIVES, DRIED CHINESE (Larm Gock)   The Chinese olive, Canarium album, is dried with salt and used in festival and vegetarian dishes, and is eaten as sweetmeat.

ONIONS   Spanish onions are best suited to Chinese cooking. Slice them thin and do not allow them to brown or become too tender. Scallions (green onions) are chopped and used as garnish.

ORANGE PEEL, DRIED   (*See* Tangerine Peel, Dried.)

OYSTER SAUCE   This delicious sauce is made from fresh oysters, but does not taste in the least like oysters. It is used for cooking meat, fish, or poultry, and is also used at the table. It is available in bottles (Ho Yo). The most popular use of it is in Beef Braised in Oyster Sauce. (*See* page 36).

OYSTERS, DRIED (Ho She)   Reddish-brown dried oysters are used to add strong flavor to soups and braised dishes. They must be soaked in cold water for 24 hours before using, then cleaned of all sand.

DEEP-FRIED STUFFED DRIED OYSTERS (Ja Yerng Ho-She):

½ lb. dried oysters
1 cup lean pork, chopped fine
1 cup shrimp, minced
1 tsp. fresh ginger root, minced
2 tsp. soya sauce

1 tsp. sugar
1 tbsp. rice wine or sherry
1 tsp. salt
Beaten egg, fine bread crumbs

Soak the dried oysters and clean. Cut each in half lengthwise. Combine the pork, shrimp, ginger, soya sauce, sugar, wine, and salt. Mix well until smooth. Spread about 1 tablespoon of this mixture on each oyster half; cover with second half. Dip the stuffed oysters in beaten egg, then roll in bread crumbs. Fry in deep fat until golden brown, about 10 minutes.

PAPER-WRAPPED CHICKEN   (*See* Chicken.)

PARSLEY, CHINESE (Een Say)   Chinese parsley has a much different and stronger flavor than the common variety. Some have described its taste as bearing a resemblance to hand-soap! But it is well worth learning to like it. It is called "fragrant green" in the native language, and is most often put into soups as a garnish.

PEA PODS (Ho Lon Dow)   Also called Chinese peas and snow peas. They are used in sautéed dishes; care must be taken not to overcook them.

PEA SPROUTS (Nga Choy)   Indeed, both the pea sprout and the bean sprout are Nature's most convenient vegetables, since they can be grown in a few days at any time of the year. Pea sprouts are grown from green mung peas, and bean sprouts (Dou Nga) from soya beans. Both are delicious and rich in vitamin C, but the pea sprout is easier to grow and more tender. The pea sprout is the type sold in Chinese markets in America, and is mistakenly referred to by most people as bean sprouts. Pea sprouts are grown as follows:

Soak 1 cup green peas (dried of course) in water for 2 to 3 days, until tiny sprouts are seen. Spread the peas out evenly between two layers of damp cheesecloth on a rack in a deep basin. Place in a dark, warm place, watering them every day, until the sprouts are 1 inch long and plump.

When ready to use, the sprouts are stirred around in a pan of cold water, whereupon the green shells (hoods) will float to the surface and can be skimmed off and discarded. The root ends of the sprouts should be trimmed off.

Important in the cooking of pea sprouts is that they not be overcooked, when they lose their crunchiness and delicate taste.

PEA SPROUTS BRAISED WITH TENDERLOIN OF PORK (Nga-Choy Chow-Yuk):

1 lb. pea sprouts	1 tbsp. soya sauce
½ lb. tenderloin of pork	1 tsp. sugar
2 tbsp. rice wine or sherry	¼ cup stock

97

Wash the pea sprouts, remove their shells, and trim the roots. Drain them well. Cut the pork into fine strips, then sauté in hot oil until lightly browned. Add the pea sprouts, wine, soya sauce, sugar, and stock. Stir, cover, and cook 2 minutes.

PEANUT OIL   (*See* Oil, Cooking.)

PEANUTS   Peanuts are favorite sweetmeats of the Chinese, and they are also used together with sesame seeds to make a kind of candy which is cut into small cubes.

PEKING DUCK   (*See* Duck, Roast.)

PEPPERS, BELL   Used in Chow Yuk dishes and very frequently in sweet and sour recipes. Green and red varieties exist.

PEPPERS, CHILI   Hot seasoning is prevalent in the cuisine of Hunan and Szechuan provinces. Hot green chili peppers are a favorite.

CHICKEN SAUTÉ WITH PEPPERS (Laht-Jew Gai-Ding):

2 pair chicken breasts, skinned	2 tbsp. soya sauce
1 lb. hot peppers, red or green	1 garlic clove, minced
1 tsp. sugar	1 cup stock

Seed the peppers and cut into 1-inch pieces. Parboil 3 minutes; drain. Cut the chicken into thin slices. Sauté the peppers for 2 minutes, then add the chicken. Add the sugar, garlic, and soya sauce. Season with salt. Add stock, cover and simmer for about 5 minutes, until chicken is just tender. Thicken the sauce with cornstarch binder.

PICKLED CABBAGE   (*See* Cabbage, Preserved.)

PICKLES, CHINESE   (*See* Tea Melon.)

PIGS' FEET   SWEET-SOUR PIGS' FEET (Sewn-Tim Jew-Shau):

3 pigs' feet	½ tsp. salt
2 tbsp. soya sauce	½ cup sugar
4 slices fresh ginger root	1 ½ cups vinegar
2 tbsp. rice wine or sherry	

Clean the feet and chop each into 4 pieces. Place in a heavy pot, add the soya sauce, ginger, wine, salt, sugar, vinegar, and enough water to barely cover. Simmer about 3 hours, or until feet are tender and sauce is thick.

PINEAPPLE   Canned pineapple is used in Chinese cooking, mostly in sweet-sour dishes.

CHICKEN WITH LITCHI & PINEAPPLE (*See* Litchi.)
SPARERIBS WITH PINEAPPLE (*See* Spareribs.)

PLUM SAUCE (So Muey Jerng)   A canned sauce prepared from plums, apricots, several other fruits, vinegar, and sugar. It is a kind of chutney served mostly with roast duck, hence it is commonly known as Duck Sauce.

PORK   Tenderloin, shoulder, and chops are the cuts of pork usually employed in quickly-cooked recipes, where the meat is cut into very small pieces. One cut of pork, which is seldom used in American cookery, except when cured, is belly pork, or un-cured bacon. It has alternating layers of lean and fat tissue, with skin on one side. In Chinese the name of this cut of meat is Five-Flower Pork (Eng Fah Yook).

CANTONESE POT ROAST (Nahm-Yew Kow-Yuk):

1 lb. fresh belly pork (Do not use cured bacon!)	2 tbsp. sugar
5 slices fresh ginger root	1 tsp. salt
¼ cup red bean curd cheese	2 tbsp. rice wine or sherry
2 tbsp. soya sauce	2 cups stock or hot water

Mix the red bean curd cheese until smooth, then add the soya sauce, sugar, salt, and wine. Cut the pork into 1-inch cubes, leaving skin on one side of each piece. Place the pork in boiling water and cook for 10 minutes. Drain well, then rub each piece with soya sauce. Brown the pork in a casserole together with the ginger. Add the prepared mixture, then stir in the stock or water. Mix well, then see that the skin side of each piece of meat is facing down, and preferably touching the bottom of the casserole. Cover and braise slowly for 2 to 2½ hours, skimming occasionally, until the fatty portion of the meat is very tender. Serve in the casserole, inverting the meat so that the skin sides are facing up.

PORK, ROAST (Cha Shew)   Cooked roast pork, prepared with spices and honey, is available in most meat markets in Chinatown. (*See* recipe on page 25.)

PRESERVED GINGER   *(See* Ginger.)

PRESSED DUCK   (*See* Duck, Preserved.)

PURPLE SEAWEED   (*See* Seaweed.)

RED BEAN SAUCE (Sharng She Jerng)   A popular canned cooking sauce, consisting of mashed red soya beans. Highly odoriferous. Used in poultry and meat dishes.

RED CHEESE   (*See* Bean Curd Cheese.)

RED DATES   (*See* Jujube, Dried.)

RED SAUCE   (*See* Sweet Vegetable Sauce, Red Bean Sauce, Bean Curd Cheese.)

RED STEWING   (*See* Cooking, Chinese Methods of.)

RED VINEGAR   (*See* Vinegar.)

RICE   Long-grained rice is preferred to oval-grained rice for texture; it is also easier to cook.

BOILED RICE:

1 cup long-grained (patna) rice   2½ cups water

Wash and drain rice. Add to water and boil for 5 minutes, stirring occasionally. Turn fire very low, cover pot, and cook for about 20 minutes. Do not uncover for first 18 minutes. When rice on top is flaky and dry, remove from heat and let stand covered for 5 to 10 minutes. Yield: 2 cups cooked rice.

STEAMED RICE:

1 cup long-grained rice   2½ cups water

Wash and drain rice. Combine with water and boil for 5 minutes. Drain off the liquid, then put rice in individual rice bowls (fill ¾ full). Place bowls on rack in large pot with 3 inches boiling water, and steam for about 75 minutes. Yield: 2 cups cooked rice.

GLUTINOUS RICE (Naw May): A short-grained, opaque rice, used in making desserts.

GLUTINOUS RICE POWDER (Naw May Fun): Used in making pastries.

ROASTING   (*See* Cooking, Chinese Methods of.)

SALTED CABBAGE   (*See* Cabbage, Preserved.)

SALTED DUCK   (*See* Duck, Preserved.)

SALTED EGGS   (*See* Eggs, Preserved.)

SALTED FISH   (*See* Fish, Salted.)

SAUCES   (*See* Bean Curd Cheese; Gravy, Chinese Brown; Oyster Sauce; Plum Sauce; Red Bean Sauce; Soya Bean Condiment; Soya Beans, Black Fermented; Soya Sauce; Sweet-Sour Sauce; Sweet Vegetable Sauce.)

SAUSAGE, CANTONESE (Lop Cherng)   These slender sausages, 6 inches long, are made from pork seasoned with wine and a hint of tangerine rind. They are tied in pairs and can be found hanging in many shops in Chinatown. They are generally sliced thin and steamed for 30 minutes.

SAUTÉING (*See* Cooking, Chinese Methods of.)

SAVORIES, HOT   (*See* Won Ton; Egg Rolls.)

SCALLIONS   (*See* Onions.)

SCALLOPS, DRIED (Gong Yew Chew)   The compressor ligament of the China Sea scallop is dried and used as a flavorful and extremely nutritious food. They can be found in Chinatown as light-brown ½-inch disks.

DRIED SCALLOPS STEAMED WITH HAM (Foh-Toy Jing Gon-Chew):

¼ lb. dried scallops	2 tbsp. onion, chopped fine
1 cup rice wine or dry sherry	1 tsp. fresh ginger root, minced
½ cup ham, chopped	½ tsp. sugar

Wash the dried scallops, then soak them for 12 hours in the wine. Drain, cut each scallop in half and arrange on a dish. Sprinkle with the ham, onion, ginger, and sugar. Place the dish in a steamer and steam for one hour.

SEASONING POWDER   This term designates any of several preparations of monosodium glutamate, under the names of Ajinomoto (Japanese), Ve-Tsin, Mee Boan (Chinese), and Ac'cent (U.S.). These whitish powders are processed from gluten, and when used prudently where the ingredients are plain, they enhance the natural taste of the other foods. Overuse creates a saccharin semblance of taste. They have no nutritious value.

SEAWEED   Two major seaweeds are used in Chinese cooking:
PURPLE LAVER (Jee Choy): Porphyra tenera. Used mostly in soup.
HAIR SEAWEED (Faht Choy): Used in vegetarian dishes and in savories.

SEAWEED SOUP (Jee-Choy Tong):

¼ lb. purple laver	1 tsp. soya sauce
1 cup ham, diced	1 tsp. seasoning powder
5 cups soup stock	Chopped scallion

Soak the laver in warm water 10 minutes. Rinse several times, until cleaned of all sand. Squeeze dry. Heat the soup stock and add the ham. Boil 5 minutes, then add the seaweed. Boil 5 minutes longer, then add the soya sauce and seasoning powder. Garnish with chopped scallion.

SESAME OIL (Jee Ma Yo)   The sesamum seed has the strongest and most delicious oil of any seed. A few drops used as garnish will improve a dish greatly. Since it is rather expensive, it is rarely used as a cooking agent. It is available bottled.

SESAME SEEDS (Jee Ma)   Sesame seeds are used in many Chinese cakes and cookies, and candies. There are two varieties available in Chinatown: WHITE SESAME SEEDS (Bock Jee-Ma), BLACK SESAME SEEDS (Ew Jee-Ma).

SHARK'S FIN (Yu Chee)   The fin of the shark, which is tasteless when fresh, is dried and exported to China from all over the world. It is extremely rich in vitamins. The preliminary preparation of the dried fin is one of many intricate stages, as follows:

Soak in water for three days. Simmer 1 hour, changing the water every 15 minutes. Simmer 3 to 4 hours longer, changing the water every 30 minutes until the skin is easily detachable. Trim the fin of any sandy skin, bone, and decayed meat. The remaining fin is of a soft yellow color. Simmer the fin for 3 hours more, until soft, but not melted into jelly. Soak in clear water until used.

Shark's fin prepared in the above manner may be obtained in Chinatown upon several days' notice. It is indeed an expensive delicacy.

SHARK'S FIN IN CHICKEN AND HAM SAUCE (Hoong-Shew Bow-Chee):

1 lb. prepared shark's fin	½ cup water
2 cups rich chicken broth	½ tsp. sugar
1 tbsp. rice wine or sherry	Soya sauce

Combine the chicken broth, chopped ham, wine, water, and 2 tablespoons soya sauce. Cover and simmer for one hour. Add the sugar during the last 10 minutes. Strain. (There should remain approximately 2 cups broth.) Pour the broth into a clean pan and add the soft, prepared shark's fin. Simmer for 10 minutes, then add one tablespoon soya sauce. Serve immediately in a very hot dish.

SHRIMP, DRIED (Ha May) Small dried shrimp are used as a strong flavoring agent in soups and stews.

SHU MAI (*See* Won Ton.)

SNAKE SQUASH (*See* Loofah Gourd.)

SNOW FUNGUS (*See* Fungus, Dried.)

SNOW PEAS (*See* Pea Pods.)

SOYA BEAN CONDIMENT (Yewn She Jerng) Variously called soy jam and brown bean sauce, this condiment is prepared from the residue left when making soya sauce. Wheat is sometimes added to the condiment, which is fermented and then called Meen She Jerng. These condiments are most commonly used in cooking fowl; also in meat dishes.

SOYA BEANS, FERMENTED BLACK (Doe She) Tiny fermented beans which are washed, crushed, and used to add a pleasant spiciness to dishes. They are often used in fish dishes to alleviate any strong smell. It is a prime ingredient in Cantonese Lobster.

SOYA JAM   (*See* Soya Bean Condiment.)

SOYA SAUCE   Soya sauce is extracted from boiled soya beans which have been salted and fermented. The general term in Cantonese for soya sauce is She Yo. There are three main subdivisions:

SHANG CHO: Light brown, fine taste, light color. Used in cooking delicate foods, where a heavy soya flavor is not desired.

CHO YO: Dark and thick, containing molasses, yet not too strong a taste. Used mostly in restaurants.

JEW YO: Most suitable for general cooking purposes and for use at the table.

Japanese soya sauce, which is prepared with the addition of malt, is much respected by the Chinese. It is readily available in the U.S.

SPARERIBS
SPARERIBS WITH PINEAPPLE (Bo-Lo Pai-Goot):

1 lb. pork spareribs	¼ cup vinegar, distilled
Soya sauce	½ cup water
1 tbsp. flour	1 cup pineapple chunks
½ cup pineapple juice	Cornstarch binder
¼ cup sugar	

Marinate the spareribs in soya sauce, drain, then sauté for 5 minutes. Stir in the flour, then add the pineapple juice, sugar, vinegar, and water. Stir, cover, and simmer for about one hour, or until ribs are tender. Season with salt. Add the pineapple chunks, heat through, then thicken the sauce with cornstarch binder.

SPINACH
SAUTÉED SPINACH, CHINESE (Chow Boh-Choy): Wash 2 pounds fresh spinach and shake off excess water. Do not cut up. Sauté in hot oil for about 3 minutes, sprinkling with salt and soya sauce to season. Do not overcook.

SPRING ROLLS   (*See* Egg Rolls.)

SQUAB (Bok Gop)   A favorite fowl of the Chinese, fresh squabs are available in Chinatown.

DEEP-FRIED SQUABS (Hoong-Shew Bok-Gop):

2 squabs	2 tbsp. rice wine or sherry
¼ cup soya sauce	1 tsp. minced fresh ginger root

Disjoint the squabs as desired. Combine the soya sauce, wine, and ginger, and rub well into the squabs. Allow to stand 30 minutes. Fry the squabs in deep fat for 10 to 15 minutes, depending on the size of the pieces. Serve on a bed of shredded lettuce.

SQUASH, CHINESE (Fon Gwa)   A small green longitudinal vegetable marrow with narrow yellow stripes.

SQUID   Fresh Squid (Yo Yew); Dried Squid (Dew Peen).

PREPARING FRESH SQUID: Pull out center bones; remove black skin. Clean out all internal organs. Cut off tentacles and reserve. Slit the squid open, then cut the meat into 2-inch squares.

PREPARING DRIED SQUID: Soak the dried squid in water for 24 hours, then clean as for fresh squid.

SQUID BRAISED WITH ONIONS AND MUSHROOMS (Hoong-Shew Dew-Peen):

1 lb. squid, fresh or dried	2 large dried black mushrooms
1 tsp. fresh minced ginger root	½ cup stock
1 tbsp. soya sauce	2 tbsp. rice wine or sherry
1 cup Spanish onion, sliced	Cornstarch binder

Clean the squid and cut into 2-inch pieces. Soak the dried mushrooms and cut into strips; squeeze dry. Sauté the squid, together with the tentacles, until the pieces curl up, about 1 minute. Add the ginger, soya sauce, and wine. Sauté 1 minute more, then remove squid to dish. Sauté onion and mushrooms, then add the stock. Cover and braise for 2 minutes. Return the squid, heat through, season with salt, then thicken with cornstarch binder. Serve immediately.

STAR ANISE   (*See* Five-Fragrance Spice Powder.)

STEAMING   (*See* Cooking, Chinese Methods of.)

STEWING   (*See* Cooking, Chinese Methods of.)

STOCK   In finer Chinese cookery, soup stock or broth is used instead of water to make the gravy of a dish. In restaurants and large homes, this stock is usually simmered from pork bones, fowl, ham, ducks' feet and miscellaneous vegetables on hand. A broth made of equal amounts of chicken and lean pork is also good. When no such freshly prepared stock is on hand, canned chicken broth is an adequate substitute. Or, in an emergency, 1 teaspoon seasoning powder to each cup of water. Stock is also used as a base for soups.

SUB GUM   Literally "miscellaneous ornament," this term is applied to a dish when the vegetable portion consists of small amounts of various vegetables.

SWALLOW'S NEST (Yeen Waw)   Some kind of seaweed is gathered by a certain specie of petrel of the family Procellariidae, which builds its nest in the cliffs of the Malayan Archipelago. The seaweed is predigested by the alkaline fluid of the mouths of these birds before being used to construct the nests. The nests are gathered in the fall, for export to China. Rich in protein, it has a delicate flavor brought out by proper cooking and seasoning. Swallow's nest is packaged in two forms, in cleaned, shallow whole nestlets, which are scarce and expensive in the U.S., and in curved chips made from the grinding of the whole nest. This is usually available in 6-ounce packages, and is expensive.

SWALLOW'S NEST SOUP, VELVET (Foo-Yung Yeen-Waw-Tong):

1 cup dry swallow's nest chips	2 egg whites, beaten until frothy
1 cup white chicken meat, minced well	1 tbsp. cornstarch
4⅓ cups rich chicken broth	¼ cup ham, chopped fine

Pour 3 cups boiling water over the swallow's nest and allow to stand overnight. Drain off the water, then place the gelatinous mass in a pan with 4 cups hot water.

Simmer for 30 minutes, then drain again. When cool, squeeze out the excess water with the hands. Pick through and discard any black feathers or impurities. Combine the finely minced chicken meat with ⅓ cup of the broth. Mix until smooth, then beat in the egg whites. Heat the 4 cups of chicken broth, add the swallow's nest, and simmer for 30 minutes. Then mix the cornstarch with a little water and stir into the soup. Correct salt seasoning if necessary. Remove the soup from the fire and slowly stir in the chicken-and-egg-white mixture. Pour the soup into a serving bowl and sprinkle with the chopped ham.

STEAMED YOUNG SQUABS STUFFED WITH SWALLOW'S NEST (Yeen-Waw Yerng Yew-Gop):

| 2 young squabs | 2 cups soup stock |
| ½ cup dry swallow's nest chips | 2 tbsp. ham, chopped |

Prepare the swallow's nest as in the preceding recipe. Squeeze dry. Slit the squabs open at the back, clean, and rub inside and out with salt. Stuff with the swallow's nest. Place the squabs, cut side up, in a bowl and pour the stock over them. Place the bowl on a rack in a large pot containing 3 inches boiling water. Cover and steam 2 hours, or until the squabs are tender. Replenish the water in the pot when necessary. Transfer the squabs to a serving dish, placing the backs down. Sprinkle with the chopped ham.

SWEET POTATO Not typically Chinese, sweet potatoes are only occasionally seen in dishes, one being Duck Braised with Yams. The potatoes are peeled, cut into 1-inch cubes and fried in deep fat until golden brown. They are then added to the braised duck. Taro is similarly employed.

SWEET-SOUR SAUCE The following is a basic recipe for use in sweet-sour dishes such as pork, shrimp, lobster and chicken:

½ cup vinegar	1 cup Chinese pickles with ginger,
½ cup sugar	sliced
1 cup water	1 tsp. soya sauce
1 tbsp. cornstarch	

Dissolve the sugar in the vinegar and water. Add the pickles. Boil 2 minutes, then add the soya sauce and cornstarch binder. Cook until thickened. To this basic sauce green peppers, tomato, pineapple, litchi, cherries, and onion may be added.

SWEET VEGETABLE SAUCE (Hoy Seen Jerng)   A canned red sauce prepared from soya beans, red rice, and garlic. It is used in preparing Peking Roast Duck, fish and shellfish dishes.

SZECHUAN PEPPER   (*See* Five-Fragrance Spice Powder.)

TANGERINE PEEL, DRIED (Gwaw Pay)   A prized subtle flavoring agent for poultry and meat dishes, imported dried tangerine peel is quite old and very expensive. It is especially used in duck recipes. It should be soaked in warm water for 15 minutes, then cleaned and rinsed.

DUCK STEWED WITH TANGERINE PEEL (Gwaw-Pay Shew-Aap):

1 tender duck	½ cup dried tangerine peel
2 pieces star anise	Boiling water
2 slices fresh ginger root	Soya sauce
1 tbsp. salt	Seasoning powder

Clean the duck and dry the outside with paper towels. Rub the skin well with soya sauce, then with peanut oil. Put the star anise inside the duck. Place the duck on a rack in a small roasting pan and put in a very hot oven until lightly browned, turning once. Remove the rack from the pan. Sprinkle the duck with the ginger, salt, and tangerine peel. Add enough boiling water to cover the duck. Put the lid on the pan and cook in a slow oven for 2 hours or longer, until the duck is tender. The broth should simmer but not boil. Remove the duck and keep warm. Strain the sauce and reduce by boiling, seasoning with soya sauce and seasoning powder. Correct salt seasoning. Thicken the sauce with cornstarch. Carve duck and arrange on shredded lettuce. Sprinkle with the reserved tangerine skin. Serve sauce separately.

TARO   Only occasionally seen in Chinese cooking. (*See* Sweet Potato.)

TEA There are three main categories of Chinese tea. GREEN TEA: The leaves are dried over a fire immediately after picking. BLACK TEA: The leaves are first allowed to ferment before roasting. RED TEA: An intermediate process.

VARIETIES OF CHINESE TEA:

Green:

DRAGON'S WELL (Lown Jeng Cha): From Hangchow. Considered the finest green tea of China. Delicious and fragrant.

CLOUD MIST (Wun Mo Cha): From Kiansi Province. The tea is grown on high mountain cliffs and monkeys are trained to pluck and gather the leaves. Delectable.

FRAGRANT PETALS (Herng Peen Cha): From Chinkiang Province. Fragrant.

WATER NYMPH (Shuy Seen Cha): From Kwangtung Province.

EYEBROWS OF LONGEVITY (Sho May Cha).

DRAGON'S BEARD (Loong So Cha).

SILVER NEEDLES (Ngun Jum Cha).

Black:

IRON KWAN YIN (Teat Goon Yum Cha): Grows on steep cliffs in Amoy. Exquisite, natural fragrance, unequalled by that of any other tea.

KEE MUN (Kee Mun Cha): Smooth and delicate.

PO NAY (Po Nay Cha): From Yunnan. A powerful tonic tea.

MO YEE (Mo Yee Cha): From Fukien Province.

CLEAR DISTANCE (Ching Yuen Cha): From Kwangtung Province.

Red:

JASMINE (Mook Lay Fa Cha).

LITCHI (Lay Jee Cha).

BLACK DRAGON (Ew Loong Cha): The tea most commonly used in homes.

Observations in Brewing Tea:

Tea is not merely a mixture of tea leaves and water. It must be made in the right strength, using ½ to 1 teaspoonful of tea leaves per cup of water, depending on the individual quality of the tea and the amount to be made, since the more boiling water is used, the larger the degree of heat upon the leaves, and consequently the stronger the infusion. Use less tea leaves per cup the larger the brew.

The teapot should be of porcelain or earthenware, never of metal. It must be warmed with boiling water before the leaves are put in.

Water used for making tea should be fresh. Never use stale water that has been allowed to stand in a kettle. In China, spring or well water is used, and even melted snow. In the U.S., one cannot hope ever to brew perfect tea with city drinking water. The water used should be heated to the bubbling point and immediately poured over the leaves in the teapot. The water must not be allowed to boil, yet if not heated enough, the tea leaves will float. Tea should be brewed for about three minutes.

The tea cups should also be warmed.

Tea must be drunk hot; lukewarm tea loses its flavor.

Tea leaves must be kept in air-tight cans, to retain their volatile oils and prevent absorption of other odors.

Unlike wine, tea does not improve with age. The finer the tea leaves, the sooner it should be used and enjoyed.

TEA MELON (Cha Gwa)   A canned, sweet cucumber pickle, amber in color and very crisp. Eaten cold as a pickle or steamed with meat.

SLICED BEEF STEAMED WITH TEA MELON (Cha-Gwa Jing Ngow-Yuk):

½ lb. tenderloin of beef	1 tbsp. soya sauce
¼ cup tea melon	½ tsp. sugar
2 tsp. cornstarch	Chopped scallion

Slice the beef thin, then combine with the cornstarch, soya sauce, and sugar. Allow to stand a few minutes, then spread evenly in a dish. Wash and slice the tea melon; arrange over the beef. Sprinkle with chopped scallion, then add a few drops of sesame oil or peanut oil. Steam 30 minutes.

TIGER LILIES   (*See* Lilies, Dried Tiger.)

TOMATO   Used in sweet-sour dishes and other sautés.

TOMATO CATSUP   Tomato catsup originated in China, as can be seen from the pronunciation of the Cantonese (Kair=Tomato; Jup=sauce). Used in some braised dishes, such as Shrimp Braised in Tomato Sauce.

TREE FUNGUS   (*See* Fungus, Dried.)

TREPANG (Hoy Sharm)   Also known as beche-de-mer, and sea-slug, the trepang, Stichopus japonicus, is available dried. It is used in soups and stews.

TURNIP ROOT, CHINESE (Got)   A root tuber, Pueraria thunbergiana, available in Chinatown.

UTENSILS, CHINESE COOKING   The following is a list of the basic cooking utensils available for sale in Chinatown:

CHINESE FRYING PAN: A convex-bottomed, circular pan of thin pounded iron or brass, ranging in size from 12 to 30 inches in diameter. Accessories for the pan are an adapter ring, for using the pan on a conventional gas range, the cover, and a bamboo brush for cleaning the pan.

STIRRING UTENSILS & LADLES: A small spatula and a pair of long wooden chopsticks are often used together for the sauté technique. A large ladle composed of wire mesh is used for draining deep-fried foods, or foods in broth. A pair of long wooden chopsticks is convenient in keeping batter-coated foods separated while deep-frying.

KNIVES: Cleavers of various sizes are used for slicing and chopping. A large assortment, all razor-sharp, is available.

STEAMERS: Large professional "steaming cages" contain trays of bamboo mesh and are used mostly in restaurants, being capable of cooking a large amount of food at one time. For home use, an ordinary large pot, with a metal rack supported by some means several inches from the bottom, is adequate. A Chinese frying pan that is large and deep enough can be used, in conjunction with a small bamboo mesh rack and cover, for steaming small dishes.

VE-TSIN   (*See* Seasoning Powder.)

VEGETABLE SAUCE   (*See* Sweet Vegetable Sauce.)

VERMICELLI   (*See* Noodles.)

VINEGAR   Chinese rice vinegar is available in Chinatown. For sweet-sour dishes, use white rice vinegar (Bok Cho) or distilled cider vinegar. Two other rice vinegars, for use at the table as dipping sauces, are:

BLACK RICE VINEGAR (Jit Cho): From Chinkiang.

RED RICE VINEGAR (Hoan Jit-Cho).

WALNUTS   Served as a sweetmeat, or used to garnish some dishes, particularly fowl.

113

WATER CHESTNUT (Ma Tuy)   The water chestnut, Trapa natans, or water caltrop, is an aquatic bulb which grows in the mud of ponds. It has a delicate flavor and a crisp texture similar to the apple. Water chestnuts are often available fresh in Chinatown (they are reddish-brown and are called "horses' hoofs" in Chinese). They also come neatly cleaned and peeled in cans, only these are somewhat expensive, yet very often worth it, since the cleaning and paring of the fresh water chestnuts is an arduous task. Water chestnuts are mostly used in Chow Yuk dishes. In China water chestnuts are made into a starch and used as a binder.

MINCED PORK STEAMED WITH WATER CHESTNUTS (Ma-Tuy Jing-Yuk):

½ lb. pork tenderloin, minced
1 cup water chestnuts,
    chopped coarsely

2 tsp. soya sauce
½ tsp. salt
1 tsp. peanut oil

Combine all ingredients and mix well. Place on a plate and form into a thin pancake. Place the plate on a rack in a pot containing 2 inches boiling water. Cover and steam for 25 minutes, or until pork is cooked.

WATER CHESTNUT FLOUR (Mah-Tuy Fun)   Made from the water caltrop and used in China as a thickening agent. It can be found in some Chinatowns here, but is fairly expensive. (*See* Cornstarch.)

WATERCRESS, CHINESE (Gwa-Jee Choy)   Unlike the common watercress, the Chinese variety has spongy oval leaves, slightly acid. Used in soups.

WHITE NUT   (*See* Gingko Nut.)

WINE, CHINESE: The cooking wine of China is rice wine, the best being from Shao Hsing. It is of a golden color, mild, and very similar to a dry sherry, which is the nearest substitute, although Japanese sake might be used. Other Chinese wines:

KAOLIANG WINE (Shew Jo): This wine is made in northern China from kaoliang, a variety of grain sorghum. It is really not a wine at all, being as strong, if not stronger. than vodka.

FRUIT RINDS & HERBS WINE (Eng Ga Pay): Slightly bitter.

ORANGE WINE (Charng Fa Low).

PEAR WINE (Sewt Lay Low).

CELERY WINE (Yun Chun Jo).

ROSE WINE (Mooi Gway Low).

CITRON WINE (Fut Show Low).

WINTER MELON (Doan Gwa)   A large vegetable marrow, Benincasa cerifera, the size and shape of a water melon, with a white frosted appearance on its light green rind. The meat is white with yellow seeds. It is used in soups and, of course, to make the well-known Winter Melon Soup. Its flavor is most delicate. Winter melon is also preserved in small cubes with sugar, as a confection and ingredient in sweet pastries and desserts. Winter melon is available fresh in Chinatown; portions of the whole melon may be purchased.

WINTER MELON AND HAM IN BROTH (Foh-Toy Doan-Gwa Tong):
 1 lb. piece winter melon   2 qt. water
 ½ lb. fine Virginia ham

Seed the melon and pare off the rind. Cut into slices ¼ by 2 inches. Cut the ham into ½-inch dice. Add the melon and ham to the cold water, heat to boiling, then simmer for ½ hour. Season with salt.

WINTER MUSHROOM   (*See* Mushrooms, Dried Chinese.)

WINTER VEGETABLE   (*See* Cabbage, Preserved.)

WON TON   Won Ton skins (Won Ton Pay) can be purchased in Chinatown by the pound. They are prepared from flour and eggs. Each skin is 8 inches square, and can be cut in quarters for Won Ton, or left whole for Egg Rolls. Each pound of skins equals 20 skins and makes 80 Won Ton. The skins are filled with a filling, meat or seafood, then folded and pinched together. They are then cooked in soup, or deep-fried and served with sweet-sour sauce, or steamed and served as a tea-time snack (Shu Mai).

FILLING FOR WON TON:

2 cups chopped chicken meat, shrimp, pork, or any combination
½ tsp. minced ginger
1 tsp. sugar
1 tbsp. soya sauce
2 tbsp. finely chopped scallion
1 tbsp. sesame oil or peanut oil
1 tsp. cornstarch

Combine all ingredients and allow to stand for 30 minutes. Place a spoonful of the filling on each skin, gather up and pinch edges together to seal in filling. Add to boiling soup stock for 1 minute, or deep-fry until golden, or steam 10 to 15 minutes.

YAM   (*See* Sweet Potato)

Index

Fish Croquettes over Braised
  Chinese Cabbage, 32
Deep-Fried Fillet of Fish Stuffed with Pork,
  Garnished with Hard-Cooked Eggs, 53
Deep-Fried Fillet of Fish in Batter
  with Sesame Seeds, 64

Abalone Braised in Oyster Sauce, 69
Abalone & Black Mushroom Soup, 69
Stewed Dried Abalone, 69
Dried Scallops Steamed with Ham, 102
Sea Scallops Steamed with Ham, 59
Curried Cantonese Crab, 80
Lobster Cantonese, 91
Deep-Fried Stuffed Dried Oysters, 96
Squid Braised with Onions & Mushrooms, 106
Shark's Fin in Chicken & Ham Sauce, 104
Fish Maw in Chicken Broth, 84

MEAT DISHES

Medallions of Pork with Crabmeat Filling, 5
Steamed Minced Pork in Whole Eggshells, 17
Hard-Cooked Eggs Deep-Fried in Minced
  Pork Coating, 23
Chinese Barbecued Pork, 25
Braised Tenderloin of Pork over Bean
  Sprouts, Egg Garnish, 42
Curried Tenderloin of Pork Braised with
  Sweet Potatoes, 47
Tenderloin of Pork Braised with
  Green Olives, 50
Tenderloin of Pork Braised with Bamboo
  Shoots & Green Peppers,
  Sweet-Sour Sauce, 55

Tenderloin of Pork Braised with
  Orange Peel, 63
Minced Pork Steamed with
  Water Chestnuts, 114

Beef Stewed in Fruit Sauce, 11
Tenderloin of Beef Braised with
  Mushrooms & Bamboo Shoots, 19
Tenderloin of Beef in Curry Sauce
  with Onions, 27
Tenderloin of Beef Braised in Oyster Sauce, 37
Beef Smoked with Fragrant Spices, 44
Beef Plate Braised in Soya Sauce, 73
Sliced Beef Steamed with Tea Melon, 112

Spareribs Barbecued with Fragrant Spices, 39
Spareribs Braised in Tomato Sauce, 61
Spareribs with Pineapple, 105
Ham Rolls with Chicken & Walnut Filling,
  Sauce with Mushrooms &
  Bamboo Shoots, 35
Breast of Lamb in Casserole,
  with Ground Rice, 38
Sweet-Sour Pigs' Feet, 99

VEGETABLE DISHES

Stuffed Chinese Black Mushrooms Steamed
  in Chicken Broth, 13
Braised Chinese Cabbage with
  Chopped Prawns, 14
Braised Stuffed Cucumbers, 31
Fresh Mushrooms Braised in Oyster Sauce, 28
Soup with White Vegetables, 51
Asparagus Braised with Beef, 70

Bamboo Shoots Braised with Sliced Breast
  of Chicken, 71
Marinated Fresh Bamboo Shoots, 71
Bean Curd with Mushrooms in
  Oyster Sauce, 72
Bean Curd Braised with Pork in
  Brown Gravy, 72
Bitter Melon Braised with Beef, 74
Chinese Cabbage Sauté, 75
Chinese Cabbage Soup, 76
Eggplant Braised with Beef, 84
Soup with Hairy Melon & Chicken, 89
Lotus Root Soup, 92
Sliced Lotus Root Braised with Pork, 92
Lotus Seeds in Chicken Broth, 93
Mustard Greens Soup, 94

Pea Sprouts Braised with
  Tenderloin of Pork, 97
Seaweed Soup, 103
Sautéed Spinach, Chinese, 105
Winter Melon & Ham in Broth, 115

MISCELLANEOUS DISHES

Frogs' Legs Braised with Winter Melon, 86
Steamed Rice Pudding with
  Preserved Fruits, 86
Snow Fungus in Chicken Broth, 87
Soup with "Powdered Silk" Vermicelli
  & Chicken, 95
Swallow's Nest Soup, Velvet, 107

57